MIDNIGHT PHOENIX MEDIA

Copyright 2023 Stephen Malins

ISBN-13: 978-0645849202

DISCLAIMER

All names have been changed and there are characters who are composites of more than one person. Some places and dates have been changed.

PART A

CHAPTER 1 EARLY DAYS

I was born in London. Many people had to be. It was a world city, after all.

You may recognise that first sentence as a paraphrase of Bill Bryson's opening in his travelogue *The Lost Continent* describing his early life in Des Moines, on the flat plains of the Midwest before he jumped in his car and drove the small towns of the US. My childhood was modest too, although I later tried my luck in a few endeavours.

I grew up in west London quite happily, but unaware of the world around me. Never mind London was a world city; an epicentre of International Finance after the "Big Bang" deregulation of 1986. As for a modest life, I am reminded of the historian AJP Taylor's "Little England"—a place where life revolved around the post office, the village and the weekly football.

As for that wider world, the Second World War had ended not even 40 years prior. The countries of Europe across the Channel were seen by my schoolmates and me through a lens of cliches, and a pastiche of old scenes from black and white war films.

So, to us, France had to be a series of cliches: bread baguettes —*pain?* men in striped shirts and berets. France, a mere 18 miles across the channel, was an exotic place. They spoke a Latin language so different to ours first introduced to us by "*Frere Jacques*" in primary school. Friends took beach holidays in the south of France, and postcards plopped on to the doormat illustrating the blue skies of the Mediterranean.

Frankly, to a ten-year-old schoolboy well versed in playing

war, Germany meant men of the Wehrmacht armed with stick grenades—in decent Hugo Boss uniforms, mind you. Even more exciting was hearing about the Royal Air Force duelling with Messerschmitt 109Bs in the Battle of Britain.

Later in life, I discovered I had an athletic bone in my body and reached out to test it. Starting with athletics at school, I joined the Army Reserve as a paratrooper and kept up training whilst studying at university. I developed a taste for a challenge mentally and physically.

My adventures as a young man are recounted in my book *A Year on Land and Sea*. By the age of 21, I had got a degree, qualified as a military parachutist, and sailed across the Atlantic Ocean. I believed life was meant to be a challenge of experience, with a bit of verve tacked on.

I graduated from university with not quite a useless Law and International Relations degree and spent a year consulting to the Defence industry which led to a job in IT. It was a start to an illustrious career, maybe.

By 1998, I found myself working for a bank in the heart of Europe, in Luxembourg City. I had an apartment, car and they paid me a *per diem* to boost my salary. I thought it an exciting place to live and work. Long two-hour lunches and ski trips were the order of the day. My flat lay in the tourist heart of the old city, at the back of the Duke's Palace, his Royal Guards within hailing distance. Place d'Armes, the main square, was literally a stone's throw away, and in winter, I threaded my way through people queuing at kiosks serving mulled wine. In summer, the denizens of Luxembourg spilled on to tables and lingered over delicious salads. The French-inspired cuisine meant lunch could be a leisurely taken steak and chips out of the office.

Luxembourg had to be a place to make movies, and I appeared in a few low-budget French-Belgian arthouse movies. Enjoying myself immensely, I was approached during a shooting break by a casting agent and asked to visit her at her office. We sat on her couch and chatted. She rang me later, asking me to read a script for a Guy Ritchie movie. I got tied up at work and missed my big break.

You might remember 2000 was a worrying year for business, when it was deemed computers all over the world were going to go haywire when they processed the flip from "99" to "00". Did this mean computers would confuse the year 2000 with 1900? Were we going to sing "Auld Lang Syne" and find large amounts of cash in our accounts, or be cleared out entirely? Those fears did not materialise, but the hours we put in stopped that disaster. A lot of companies were busy, I can tell you.

So, I got to Europe and broadened my horizons after all.

I used the opportunity to visit the cities of Western Europe. Eastern Europe lay further away though, and I still needed to be back at work at 9 am on the Monday, and do my washing on Sunday night, which limited even the most ambitious. I flew back to London at the weekends occasionally to see my parents and start my car. I told this story with a suppressed grin until people were sick of it.

I bought a flat in a cheap south London suburb, pleased it was on a railway line. I was not so cheered to feel the heavy goods trains rattling past. Friends gloated they had bought near Tooting Broadway on the Northern line Tube, but it got me a start on the housing ladder which was going berserk. There had been a huge price increase in 1999, and people were piling in. No one knew how long prices would climb for, but people buckled themselves in for the ride.

The flat occupied the upper floor of a two-storey block, four in total. It was nice to have a second bedroom, but I found the location underwhelming. Rubbish was often dumped on a street corner near the railway line. Still, I had that foothold. It was all part of the gritty experience of South London, and many of us youngsters in reasonably well-paid jobs found ourselves priced out of the nicer parts.

In 1999, I decided I would escape Europe for a week somewhere *ambitious*—and jotted place names on a shortlist which I narrowed down to California and South Africa. Australia was my first choice. My cousin and his family left west London in the early 1990s to head to Sydney, and their postcards painted an endless ideal of a superior life.

"It's too far," said my colleague. "The jet lag will kill you."

I reckoned I could deal with the travel and the jet lag—but there would be little time to do anything. The convenience of California took line honours, and I shelved my ambition to get "Down Under".

My hand was turned, though. 2000 might have worked out, but 2001 brought the shock of 9/11. A mini-recession hit Europe and my consulting company started down-sizing. I hadn't given up on my ambition altogether to get to Australia, and when I realised I could get a Working Holiday visa, I applied for redundancy, hoping to get there before I turned 30 years old.

I got the redundancy I asked for. I met my local HR rep, who turned up with a sympathetic look on her face. The room set aside for her news had the air of a funeral parlour, and she introduced herself in hushed tones. She didn't know I had asked for redundancy, and when she saw me, sitting there relaxed and pleased, her demeanour changed. She cooed at my plans and explained the terms of the payment. It got a bump from all the annual leave I hadn't taken.

I arrived in Sydney with a large bank balance, which I kept quiet about. You could say I sat comfortably in the upper echelons of the *Top 100 Rich Backpacker's List*—if one ever existed.

The fact of the matter is that I rather took to my year in Australia in my sabbatical. I uncovered real life far from the hustle and bustle of the beaches and coffee shops on the east coast. I learned to fly, and worked on sheep and cattle stations, passed a truck test by the skin of my teeth—and toiled out in the gold fields in 40-degree heat.

I made it out west and a mate joined from the UK. We hired two planes in a syndicate with other pilots. We flew ourselves around the south west corner and then a girl I'd met and I drove to Alice Springs along the coast of the north-west via Katherine. You can read all about this in my book, *Rah Rah and Roos* (2020). I also uncovered the fact that the flip-flops you wore on your feet were called *thongs*. British people thought this highly amusing.

In that year, I came to see the country, the only country that is also a continent and an island. I didn't just ply the coast, though. I stayed with family friends in a small subtropical town and saw the real Australia.

When I wasn't on the road, I enjoyed the wall-to-wall sunshine of Sydney—even winter seemed gloriously sunny, as my emails home recounted in a sort of gloat, if truth be told.

I loved the beaches and the sport. Maybe I had fancy ideas, but I worked out I could live there; the possibilities seemed endless. After the travails of my twenties, training, and work, Sydney seemed to represent a more meaningful life, a better work-life balance. I felt optimistic.

I returned to London in 2003 when my visa ran out and braved the end of winter, noticing the low-lying cloud and purple sky when I wheeled my suitcase to the taxi rank. It seemed as if the sky had collapsed in on me. Those first few weeks back, though, I appreciated the sense of the "old world" and culture. I went back to work. I had turned 30 years old.

Spring arrived, and 2003 turned out to be a better summer, even surpassing records. In August, it hit 32 degrees and Londoners on the Tube and in offices throughout the capital sweltered without air conditioning. I had a master plan to head back to Sydney. I had used the darker nights there to fill in a migration application form. Waiting times could be up to a year, but I was fast-tracked, and my passport returned by post with a visa glued in a blank page.

In a delightful turn of events, I also met my wife. She had trained as a professional dancer and worked as a pilates instructor at a top-flight studio. We met at a friend's house one Sunday morning. I admired her form and her evident beauty. To my dismay, she left in a Porsche 911 belonging to someone who had been at brunch with us, and I figured that would be the end of it. I worked her friend shamelessly so I could seize the chance to see her again.

Kiki and I met at a pub with our friends and talked all evening. Later, we met for a date on Southbank under Waterloo bridge. We were engaged months later in a one-star Michelin restaurant I had scoped in the high street. I cadged a bottle of wine from the owner who agreed to be a complicit accomplice. We were seated close to another couple in the corner, so I couldn't get down on one knee (less pressure, perhaps). I presented her with a beautiful diamond from a dealer contact in Hatton Garden, perfect in every way, other than size. The gentleman pricked up his ears when I popped the question. Maybe he thought I was asking him.

We studied the paperwork accompanying the diamond. It was one-quarter of a carat—small, yes, but also somewhat perfect. Beautiful things came in small packages, after all. The insured value: three times what I paid for it.

Kiki knew I had been meaning to return to Sydney, so when we got engaged, we both knew what lay in store. We were both getting two adventures for the price of one. You can see it as a huge gamble, or a romantic new interlude. I saw it as the latter, and never considered for a moment it not working out.

CHAPTER 2 FORGET WHAT JEREMY CLARKSON SAYS

Australia.

It was first brought to my attention by the TV show *Neighbours,* which featured in the daily lives of most of my school friends in the 1980s. Not that I watched it, but I heard about Scott and Charlene's wedding, and tuned in accidentally on a school-night to see the stunning Jane emerge after her makeover. She had been hidden under a frumpy 80s gown and a pair of glasses. Lipstick and the removal of the specs did wonders.

When I turned twelve, we had a boy start in my year, and we saw his natural athleticism. With nods all-round, we saw he could throw a javelin any distance at all, when none of us could. (It once flew true through the air and narrowly missed our headmaster's head as he strode the pitch towards one of his teachers.) We could have been jealous, but we were relieved a boy knew what they were doing.

The word was he had been brought up in Australia. That changed things. We considered him to be the anointed one. He backed up prowess in the Field with sublime rugby skills and could kick goals, too. We could only dream of being able to slot a ball through the uprights. This lent credence to the fact that not only was Australia exotic, but it also bred supermen.

I found myself enthralled by their sporting excellence. I recall the time as an 18-year-old sitting to watch England play Australia in the 1991 Rugby World Cup Final broadcast down the road at Twickenham. Having got that far playing in a boring style, England tried to play a running game and lost. The Australians in their gold tops and green shorts proudly held aloft the William Ellis trophy.

When it came to *Australis*, the "Great Southern Land", people of my parent's age might have thought of Christmas on the beach —the seasons reversed—or even, kangaroos skipping down the main street, which they do, in places. Even in my cousin's street.

Skippy the Kangaroo repeats ran on the television a bit before my time. I remembered *Sons and Daughters* and *A Country Practice*. The classic *Prisoner Cell Block "H"* came on later at night and depicted a rough crowd of women in a prison laundry. I hadn't realised entire tv serials were Australian, imagine that.

From the 1960s onwards, Australia accepted migrants from the UK (and other places too) and one such initiative saw thousands leaving English ports by sea for a new life. Many of these were known as "Ten Pound" Poms. I considered myself to be a "One Thousand Pound Pom" at 2003 prices. I paid £700 for the visa application—and £300 for the one-way airfare. The medical cost me £100, so let's call it a round £1,000.

Many "Ten Pound" Poms were accommodated in Nissan-style metal huts in places like Nunnawading in the eastern suburbs of Melbourne before they bought or signed up for new house-and-land packages after getting regular employment. No doubt many regretted their decision, but having come all that way, there would have been an incentive to stick with it. There were later stories of migrants having arrived by air, not liking what they saw in the taxi into town asking to be returned to the airport. This story is not necessarily apocryphal. I consider it to be true.

Jeremy Clarkson from the popular TV show *Top Gear* once said no one of any consequence ever went to Australia. This does back a view for all Australia's marvels, it *was* a backwater, a back corner, situated neither in Asia nor in Europe. It had been considered the "trash" of Asia, and Bob Hawke, the famous Australian Prime Minister in the 1980s, talked of a "Banana Republic."

A friend didn't seem impressed either, and reading between

the lines, she probably thought I had a colonial view of the world and wanted to escape Europe's increasing influx of migrants (an excuse many a migrant had made). But moving to Australia meant I was a migrant too.

Australia had started out, of course, as a penal colony. The British First Fleet sent to settle Australia comprised convicts, their wardens, and a class of administrators and leaders. This had been described in Robert Hughes's seminal *The Fatal Shore*, one of Australia's finest art critics and historians.

People seemed split on Australia. For some, it seemed to represent a dream location, a paradise yearned for. But it lay a long way from anywhere, and even in 2002, the year I arrived, it took a good 24 hours to get to Sydney regardless of whether you travelled via Asia, or the US, whichever way you circled the world.

It definitely held a fascination for the Brits. I suspect this is to do with the weather and the fact people spoke English. Brits attributed a certain character to the Australians; an admiration for the plucky, no-nonsense character we had seen on display in the soaps where it always seemed to be summer, and no one ever fell out with each other for long. People considered Australians good sports, down-to-earth, and fortunate.

I had come across a well-known book, *The Lucky Country* by Donald Horner written in the 1960s, although it often gets forgotten in the noise. Never mind, the book's title was ironic and set out to be a critique of Australia. The fact remains, the label stuck.

We found the TV awash with programmes about people moving to Australia, or Spain. *Escape To the Sun* proved popular, and the host met families down there and shadowed them through the first days. Brits had long headed south to try their luck. I suppose a European country might have been an option, but my lack of fluency in a language had to be an obstacle.

You wouldn't catch me lying on a beach for hours, but I appreciated the crescent-shaped sand vistas of many I saw. We had the chance to buy a house, maybe with land. We weren't interested in a majestic pile, a farm, a vineyard, or even a reno. The goal: to have a backyard, or *bush*, and think about a family.

CHAPTER 3 GATEWAY TO A NEW LIFE

Kiki came from a large, interesting family, far more so than my own. It sprawled across the Americas and Europe, and she had regaled me with stories of her brothers and sisters. She was born in Mexico City, of Italian-Spanish ancestry, but had come of age in Scotland. She had the bright idea of introducing me to her family *on the way* to Sydney, so we booked to go via the US.

"We'll get a larger baggage allowance," I noted to her, thinking practically. "We can take two suitcases up to 50 pounds each."

This had to be better than the single 20 kilogramme (44lb) limit we got going via Asia, so that was a win there, getting belongings over.

On Christmas Day, 2003, friends dropped us off at Heathrow Airport and we boarded a flight to San Francisco. I counted myself lucky to have seen a bit of the US already. I had been to the east coast to toil on a summer camp in 1995. In 1999, a Californian road trip took me to LA, Las Vegas, and San Francisco, with a sideshow to the Grand Canyon. After the road trip, I'd got to a Thanksgiving dinner in Boston to see a mate. We hiked Mount Washington in New Hampshire, camped in blustering winds, and on the way down bumped a large moose resting in a clearing. This was my *second* visit then, to California, a fact I reminded my fiancée repeatedly—*there were no flies on me*.

Our port of entry: San Francisco, but my fiancée's family lived further down the Bay Area in the Valley. I had heard of Silicon Valley, the home to IT and emerging Tech. I found this a novelty. For some reason, I had convinced myself Silicon Valley an overflow of *Los Angeles*. Still, you live and learn. The area enjoyed the service of the Bay Area Rapid Transit (BART), a phrase I took to immediately, and I liked the way it sounded when I tried it out in my head. *The Simpsons* came to mind.

We arrived in a winter in Silicon Valley, but the sun shone, and I liked it from the get-go. The drive from the airport took the main highway from San Francisco along the bay with smudgy hills in the distance. We passed Mountain View, Palo Alto—a litany, or *Who's Who* of tech place names. Everything was "super" convenient (I had never used the word super like that. I reserved it for comic book characters with powers, like Superman.)

Kiki introduced me to her parents, and brothers and sisters, and for a short, heady time I purred, the centre of attention, until they had worked me out. They were probably sizing us up for a sweepstake and submitting bets for how long the union would last.

Family life centred in a classic detached house in a side street off a main route through the valley, with cream weatherboard panels and a shingled roof. I found a Corvette parked in the street, and admired a Mustang, typical enough for the US, but turned the corner and found the main headquarters of eBay.

We visited the shopping malls and places to eat dotted around. Taking advantage of the exchange rate and prices, we looked for bargains at an electrical super store. We loitered at a display of cameras and bought a new digital compact. They were still relatively new. With *three* entire megapixels on board, it seemed to meet a need to document our new life.

We drove to San Francisco, and had dinner in a restaurant there, and I learnt a little Spanish. In a moment of comedy, which I arranged, I asked my brother-in-law to translate for my father-in-law when I asked for his permission to marry. He smiled, granted it, and seemed to forgive the cringe factor I had introduced.

There were lots of breakfast options, US-style. We tried sugared cereal, bagels and sipped orange juice out of gallon-sized bottles. I tried a Danish pastry one morning.

"You want milk with that?" asked my soon to be brother-in-law, joining me.

I saw his curiosity in Australia. While he munched on a bowl of Trader Joe's cereal, I gave him an idea of the sheer scale of the land.

If you overlapped Australia on to Europe, she extended from the tip of Portugal in the west to the edge of Russia in the east. I explained most of the population lived along the east coast but concentrated in an arc in the south-east corner in Sydney and Melbourne. He had heard of the Great Barrier Reef in Queensland, "Beautiful One Day, Perfect the Next." I told him the sea met the rain forest north of Cairns at Port Douglas, yet on the other side of the country, the mining city of Perth sat on its own —closer to Singapore than Sydney.

Kiki's sister helped us to the airport for our trip to Sydney. Mindful of my luggage allowance, I had on several coats to keep my baggage weight down. I put up, and shut up, with the rising warmth as we stood in the queue.

We arrived at the gate and spotted our jumbo 747 operated by Qantas. The airline had commissioned the words "The Spirit of Australia" enticingly on the side, not that we needed more encouragement to board. The flight from the West Coast of the US to the east coast of Australia across the Pacific looked to be a marathon. Neither of us had ever leapt-frogged the Pacific Ocean before, or flown for so long.

Seatbelt secured across my hips, I peered at the flight path in the glossy magazine and noted the islands with runways we could divert to. Fiji and Vanuatu were dead certs, but many specks were barely bigger than an atoll. Hawaii sat about halfway, much closer, but so far, too.

Being good sports, we ate the food presented to us, watched movies and slept in fitful episodes, our blankets tucked under our chins. As we came into land in Sydney, in New South Wales, I remembered doing the same two years ago, coming in from Singapore. I felt a heady sense of excitement. Kiki leant over and held my hand, sensing the magnitude of the moment. It worked on two accounts; the first she knew we were returning to a special place I had lived in and loved, and the start of a new life together. It had to be a sweet moment.

I pointed out the city skyscrapers on the harbour. Known by millions from photos, the waters divided the Emerald City. The Sydney Harbour Bridge—the "coat hanger"—provided a road and rail crossing, with the iconic opera house completed in 1973, glistening in the sunshine alongside. I couldn't imagine a Sydney without it. First-time visitors telling you it's smaller inside than expected are just poo-pooing on your parade.

Accounting for the fact we crossed the international dateline, and the full day we lost, we landed just before New Year's Eve. The brilliant blue sunshine leaked in through the windows and poured into the aisle.

I let Kiki go through migration first as a tourist, then as a new permanent resident, offered my passport to the officer. Understand, though, I had my cover story all ready to go.

I expected her to push a panic button and detain me on the spot. After all, it was a little-known fact I had been banned from Australia, but surely *immigration* knew.

For my year backpacking, I had a working holiday visa, but there had been a problem. Australia House in the Strand had transposed a digit in my passport number on the visa. It did not flag in Dubai when a member of the Qantas ground crew checked my passport. He thought he had been doing me a favour when he issued me a three-month tourist visa. It would have been nice if he had told me.

I landed in Sydney not knowing I had months, rather than a year. The situation unravelled the day I left Australia as I presented myself at migration. The agent scratched her head and asked me to follow her to an office. My nonchalance soon wavered when she said:

"Fault or no fault, you're banned from Australia for three years."

I sat through the flight to London in a daze. The next morning, I rushed to Australia House. A girl there put my mind to rest.

"It's ok. It's a ban on a tourist visa. Your application for a

Permanent visa still stands—you can enter on that."

So here at arrivals, I wasn't detained, nor deported. Imagine if Kiki had been left alone to show herself around our new home.

CHAPTER 4 THE EMERALD CITY

It felt balmier than I had remembered, as if the humidity had been dialled up especially for us. We'd checked the forecast before we left San Francisco, and the temperature would peak at 30 degrees Centigrade.

Kiki enthused about the Australian accents she could now hear, starting at the car hire desk, and looked at the sunlit city. We headed from Kingswood-Smith airport—named after an early intrepid 20th century aviator, into the summer brightness. Our destination: Coogee beach, the place I had headed for two years ago.

Harbour-side and beach living was where it was at. Residents eked out a charmed existence at landmarks like Point Piper and Watson's Bay, where they could get home from work and enjoy the harbour. Robert Hughes, also Art Editor for *Time* magazine, had written about his boyhood fishing on the harbour in his autobiography *Things I Didn't Know*. He remembered the long hot summers of his childhood—only the wetter ones of mine stuck with me. My parents though, remembered the hot one of 1976, when standpipes operated in the streets.

But the most famous beach in Australia is Bondi, pronounced "Bond-I", on the Eastern Beaches. We could see it as a quintessential city beach. Patrolling lifeguards wore highly visible red Speedo swim briefs and orange swim hats. The action doesn't stop on the sands or the surf—at Bondi Icebergs, a swimming pool in the cliff, swimmers completed lengths with the water of the Pacific tantalisingly below. The ocean spray splashed the pool, reminding swimmers they were close to nature.

Coogee sat two miles to the south of its more popular sister Bondi, but I preferred its intimacy. We pulled up on the promenade and I looked with affection at the beach and plaza, seeing strollers and swimmers. Many wore their costumes un-self-consciously into shops, their hair flicking water on the floor. I had spent six weeks living here, and I ticked off all the sights and sounds I had remembered, but Kiki found it all new.

The view of the ocean helped with the jetlag and the aches and pains of the flight. We ventured on to the beach, and took off our sandals, feeling the sand between our toes, and Kiki stepped wearily into the shallows.

I showed her two flags on the beach and repeated the mantra, "Swim between the Flags". Rips, nasty currents of water, were common, and the flags showed the safest spot. Swimmers trapped in a rip taking them out to sea should swim across to calmer waters and not fight it. The rip would invariably win.

"What about sharks?" she asked, turning to me. "That's what worries me."

I knew she'd ask. The Great White, or "White Pointer" came to mind.

"There might be a few Great Whites out there," I replied. She looked alarmed.

"But they have shark nets now," I reassured her.

"Thank God for that."

I could she wasn't convinced.

There had been fatalities over the years. Sharks confused swimmers with seals, but a prospecting bite was not trivial. Surfers could die from blood loss from a laceration.

In 1963, a young man called Rodney Fox was attacked in South Australia and he became a national poster boy. There's a well-known photo of the injury—a bite mark a foot wide across his back. He became a world authority on Great Whites and advised Stephen Spielberg for the 1970s movie *Jaws*. I thought I'd continue the theme.

"Just be glad we're not in Brisbane up north. They have Bull sharks," I said.

"*Bulls*?" her eyebrows raised.

"Yup, very dangerous, they are renowned for heading into the river."

But you needed a sense of perspective, and it needn't deter you from the water.

"Just be glad there are no crocodiles down here. They'd snap through the shark nets just like that," I continued.

Kiki's eyebrows shot higher still.

In the Northern Territory, saltwater crocodiles provided terror there, but none ventured south to temperate waters. Besides, we needed to share the danger around a bit. The box jellyfish up in tropical Queensland: now they were nasty.

"In Queensland, they close the beach in the summer months, as the 'stingers' are so dangerous."

Kiki fell silent on this one.

It was getting warm. The UV index would top out at a high of 13 by mid-afternoon, or *arvo* as they said here. When I knew the UV on a June day in London limped to six, this was no understatement. In my boyhood, Australians and New Zealanders had suffered as one when the gaping hole in the ozone layer left them wide open to skin cancers. The hole closed after CFCs used in refrigerators and aerosols were phased out in the 1980s. It had to be an early, triumphant salvo in the climate change wars.

We enjoyed the late afternoon, free from the shackles of winter. We sauntered the beach road, browsing in boutiques and shops, glancing in real estate windows. Everything seemed newer than the London we had left behind. The pavements were clean, the kerbs smooth, and awnings over each shop provided relief from the sunlight. I left Kiki to pop to the bank and found her again in a boutique in mid-purchase of a rather fetching hat. We ventured a little way down the beach path towards Clovelly beach. Despite the journey, we found it hard getting to sleep that first night in our hotel.

***

We enjoyed breakfast, looked after by an ever-obliging waitress who smiled through perfect teeth and said "No Worries" a lot.

We caught the bus into town, aiming to catch the ferry from Central Quay to Manly. We'd find that on the Upper North Shore. A ferry cruise was fun for any visitor on the trip between there and the CBD. ("Central Business District", I said.)

The Opera House lay nearby, so we sidetracked there. We strolled along the embankment from the wharves past restaurants to an outcrop of land on the water. The Harbour Bridge ran to the left along the water's edge. Up close, at the very end, we found the house not so white after all. The huge sails postured into the sky like petals opening on a brilliant spring day after rain. Steps soared to the entrance and a concrete plaza brimmed full of tourists lazing around. The Royal Botanic Gardens spilled over to the right and provided shade.

The North Shore provided a playground, and glitz for the wealthy. The Prime Minister lived on a promontory at Kirribili House, flanked by the waterside mansions of the privileged, prominent businessmen, celebrities, and old money. This side of town represented the desirable side. Ask a debutante where she comes from, and she'd say, artfully, "North Shore" without hesitation. Palm Beach provided the location for the well-known TV show *Home and Away.*

On the ferry, we had all the time in the world, but it would have been a grand way to get to work on a Monday morning for a 9 am start. We stood at the prow watching the bow wave of the ferry as she carved through the waters.

Kiki wanted to meet an old friend from the UK. The friend had words of advice and grabbed my mobile number. We found a lovely café on a narrow road with harbour views and spent a glorious hour with the newspapers—the *Sydney Morning Herald* (the "SMH") with coffee and a meal. Evidently, the café had been shoe-horned into a space surrounded by colonial-era residences with tiny paths to front doors, and locals turned up with little dogs seeking regular spots. Judging by expressions, they appeared rather snooty, even haughty, almost Parisian in attitude. We were the *blow-ins*, the outsiders.

CHAPTER 5 NEW YEAR'S EVE

N ew Year's Eve.

Kiki and I walked with the crowds down George Street towards the Marriott hotel. My cousin and his wife, with their three children, had taken a room for the fireworks and my aunt and uncle had joined. There were also friends from London.

My cousin had booked for a commanding view of the harbour fireworks scheduled for midnight, and we congratulated him on the view and grazed on *hors d'oeuvres*. The streets and gardens along the shore were busy with families, youngsters hoisted on shoulders. The bridge featured again in the backdrop against a starry sky. I knew away from the city lights, we'd see the Milky Way in a fashion we didn't from London. It presented far more iridescent, expansive, more complex. But for now, we feasted on the fireworks whizzing and careening above the bridge as the clock struck midnight.

My cousin lived on a beach on the Central Coast of New South Wales. It lay 90 minutes from Central Railway station, and the train left the Sydney suburbs and took you through lakes and inland water ways. People commuted from out that way daily, exchanging time for the chance to live in a mini paradise.

But Kiki and I drove up for lunch. My cousin lived in a home on a rise high above town. It sprawled topsy-turvy on two levels, bedrooms downstairs. They shared the land with bush turkeys that scratched around at night.

It came of no surprise the beaches in this quiet backwater were as good as down south. One was overlooked by a hill which rose above the head a hundred metres, a grass meadow continuing to the crest, a favourite of dogwalkers. If a local tired of the beaches, they could retire for a drink at a local hotel as if in a holiday resort. I once met an older gent in a pub who called it

"God's Own Playground." Was he now in God's waiting room?

Back in Sydney, Darling Harbour looked like it might be fun. A ritzy entertainment hub on the south side of the harbour to the left of the bridge as you looked from the city. For entertainment value, it might have been a foil to the Opera House's épée. We booked a room at the Star Casino and our room looked out to the harbour where boats floated lazily at moorings. We changed for dinner and sat with a drink in the anteroom.

Sight-seeing had to be all very well, but we had come to Sydney to prospect. Kiki was here "Down Under" to see if she could get on with it. Did it pique her interest? We had agreed she could pull the plug if she got wet feet, and we could set up in London. I floated the question over drinks in the bar.

"What do you think?" I asked.

The answer was a yes.

"I'm selling my flat, too," she added.

***

I wanted to build a foundation for when Kiki returned. How do you eat an elephant? You start one bite at a time. If we were a startup, pitching to a venture capitalist, we'd have to meet milestones. I didn't see a job as high stakes, but I needed a car and a place to stay.

But transport first. I had in mind a *ute*, a "pickup" or truck, as Americans know them by. I had seen them everywhere in my gap year, travelling around the cities and the outback, and I loved their versatility—truly "a man for all seasons". Never mind I didn't plan on taking up tools as a tradesman, or *tradie;* I saw the practical side.

Australia invented the utility, strictly speaking a car with a tray on the back, not the truck the Americans knew. Holden, the Australian manufacturer (an off shoot of General Motors) first made one after the Second World War. Hardly a year went by since then when Ford or Holden hadn't made one.

Like Americans, Australians liked the pickup, often in the

guise of the ubiquitous Toyota Hilux. Jeremy Clarkson had used one on *Top Gear*, but even ten-year-old models held their price.

Parramatta Road in Sydney's west held a sizeable share of the city's second-hand dealers' yards. I peered into windows, a hand cupped over my brow, to look at odometers, and noted a white truck would reflect the heat of an Antipodean sun more so than a navy one. Keeping to the shade where possible, I stumbled on a Mitsubishi Triton on a forecourt. It was ten years old, with only one former owner—the Australian Defence force (ADF). One *careful* owner? I knew enough about defence to surmise this truck had probably not been off-road, let alone off-base. The service history seemed legit. Priced to sell at $11,500, I haggled down to $9,999.

What's striking about selling cars in Australia is you don't need a mechanic's test, or a *Roadworthy Certificate* in many states or jurisdictions. New South Wales had strict rules though, so a seller provided the buyer with a *"pink slip"*. This didn't warrant the car as being in tip-top condition, just that it was safe—free of serious rust, and had brakes, tyres and suspension in good order. In other states like Western Australia, you bought and sold "as seen". I'd seen backpackers buying South Australian cars to stay clear of red tape.

Only New South Wales required you to get your car inspected every year in order to maintain the vehicle registration. I found this astonishing. This utility had *rego* (registration) left, so the annual fee was not due.

The dealer showed me the pink slip and pointed to a bank across the road. With my passport, I found it a breeze withdrawing cash. Kiki grinned when I turned up with our white "truck".

Kiki wanted to get back to work in London and sell her flat. I drove her to the airport for her flight to the US.

"I'm seeing my sister in San Diego on the way back over. We'll get married in Mexico later in the year!" she reminded me.

We bid goodbye, hugged, and she wished me good luck. I had a challenge ahead of me, but not one I thought insurmountable. I needed to find somewhere to live, a job, when I had minimal local work experience, and sort out a base we could build from. We had both turned 30. We had plenty to get on with in this new life together. It was exciting and enthralling. I felt enterprising enough that I knew I could make it happen. I never doubted myself for a moment.

CHAPTER 6 THE MOVE SOUTH

The first shock decision we had made was to move south to Melbourne, in Victoria, and not set up in the "Emerald City" after all.

A big reason was the price of housing. Prices in Australia had risen after the Sydney Olympics in 2000, and just like in the Europe we had left behind, the nation had been caught up in its own housing boom. By the start of 2004, a family home two hours from Sydney approached $500,000, and I didn't fancy the thought of a commute from the Central Coast, even if that travel finished with a view of the Harbour.

Fierce rivalry had been a talking point between the two Premier cities in Australia. Melbourne, Australia's second city, had lower house prices, yet had as much opportunity as befitted a place with over three million people. The city is sited in circular Port Phillip Bay, and the city's suburbs and delights creep down the ever popular "Peninsula" alongside the bay for the two hours it takes to drive the coastal road. The eye could feast on the brilliant beaches and the holiday homes, or weekenders, of the wealthy with waterfront views.

For many, Melbourne seemed to play second fiddle to Sydney, which sounds contentious. It didn't quite have the glitz of the Harbour city, and in fact, until recently, I hadn't even heard of it. The city was the birthplace of Kylie Minogue, and I twigged my childhood show *Neighbours* had been filmed there.

Melbourne lacked the harbour to be fair and maybe lacked that razzle-dazzle factor. Its Central Business District (CBD) sited on the "brown" Yarra River couldn't rival Sydney's sparkling waters. I met Australians who said it couldn't match Sydney. I met many others who preferred Melbourne, not fooled by Sydney's bright lights. This was bourne out by the amusing saying: "Sydney is the girl you date, Melbourne is the girl you marry". Melbourne had *longevity*.

It had a reputation for "Four seasons in one day", especially in spring, and winters were the coldest on the Australian mainland. Winters struggle to get above 13 degrees Centigrade. In Sydney, the day slowly warmed to 19 degrees under wall-to-wall glorious sunshine.

For all the Sydney versus Melbourne rivalry, no one should frame the city in too negative a light. It would give the city a great disservice it does not deserve. It regularly topped the Economist Intelligence Unit's "Most Liveable City" table. Only Vancouver came close. It may have seemed colder in winter, but there were vineyards and beaches, front and back of the bay, and tantalising wineries. Melbourne had weather extremes, so it did enjoy warm summers. "*God*, it gets hot!" a friend had exclaimed.

I had seen photos of the city beaches in Melbourne, and many were plain gorgeous and matched those of Sydney easily, with aquamarine waters and white sands. Even a half-decent photographer could capture a shot of Brighton beach, south-east of the city, with its stunning parade of brightly coloured beach huts on the shore set against the vista of city skyscrapers in the background.

Kiki's family seemed to think there was more culture down there. St Kilda beach, a tram ride from the centre, was a vibrant place for locals and tourists alike. Ackland Street had cake shops and cafes and entertained backpackers and residents who lived in high-rise towers. People referred to Melbourne as the "Sporting capital". It had stolen the Grand Prix from Adelaide a few years before, and one of tennis's four Grand Slams was televised to a worldwide audience from Rod Laver arena.

There's a running joke Melbournians would turn a funeral into a day out. This leads to another observation I've heard the locals wear black in winter, provenance not known. (I can't say I ever noticed this myself, and I'm coming up to my 19th winter here.)

In my visit in 2002, I had found the city boiling hot, then cold, too, yes. But the scale of stuff to do had to be a draw. The entire city and inner south, north and east contained bars, eateries, and restaurants. A theatre area district ran the international shows, and streets were closed for jaunty festivals. It was a modern city with plenty to do. It would take years to exhaust it all.

And with all the time I had in the world, driving there to have a look had to be a no-brainer.

CHAPTER 7 DRIVING DOWN

To get there: two likely routes presented. One headed down the Hume Highway, over 850 kilometres, or 500 miles, nine hours along a tedious inland highway which followed sections of the railway line. It was at least dual carriageway, and the driver shared this road with trucks plying between Sydney and Melbourne.

The other took the coast road around the corner of the south-eastern hump of Australia. This was the route I favoured. It would be longer going at 640 miles, over 1,000 km, and windier, but prettier for sure, and more interesting for someone like me in no rush to be anywhere.

I planned to take the road less travelled.

Outside cities, the expansive, and expanding metropolitan area fades to natural borders such as the Blue Mountains in Sydney or extends to hills or farmland in Victoria. There are regional cities inland, like Wagga Wagga in New South Wales, and Bendigo and the gold rush town of Ballarat in Victoria. You'll hear them described as "large country towns". Albury–Wodonga on the border between New South and Victoria straddles the river, one city in *each* state.

My route won't take me anywhere near these historic places, or to "the regions". It will pass places like Bateman's Bay, Nowra, Bega, and eventually reach the Victorian border. New South Welshmen called Victorians "Mexicans".

The "4 and 20" pies in the pie warmer looked good at the service station. Correction: *servo*. The horizon shimmered already, and I could see it was shaping to be a hot day. I shared the apron with men who had pulled up with boats lashed down to trailers and busied themselves filling fuel tanks. I squinted at the price board as I filled my fuel tank. I found myself on the hook for 89 cents a litre of diesel, but a tank would get me most of the way to Melbourne. Petrol was $1.14 a litre. That had to be half-price when I paid £1 in London.

I delighted in the fact ice was available from large external cabinets, and a sign reminded me I could get barbeque gas in bottles on a "swap and go" basis.

So victualled, I got on the highway. The road out of Sydney was busy and snaked south through the well-known beach suburb of Cronulla, home to the Premiership Rugby League team: the lauded Cronulla Sharks, or "Sharkies". As I write in 2022, the Australian Prime Minister Scott Morrison has just lost the election, but he was the "No One" ticket holder for the team, their celebrity, and he's often seen at games. But he's gone.

The region south of Sydney is called the "Shire", as it sits in a local government area called Sunderland Shire. It's the kind of place traditional suburban families bring up God-fearing families. Analogous to the *Lord of the Rings* narrative, it had a safe, tranquil reputation.

I left the shire, like a modern-day Bilbo Baggins, and turned course from due south to a south-westerly direction, heading towards Wollongong, or the "Gong" a coastal city a few hours away. Checking my map at a junction, I realised Canberra lay three hours west.

Here I could find Government house, the seat of government. It's the heart of Federal politics, the top-tier of government in Australia. If I took that inland highway, I'd be in time to sign the visitor's book or even pop to the public gallery to listen to proceedings if I felt so inclined—but I pressed on, past from beach towns and signposts to "Southern Highland" destinations, tantalisingly signposted from the highway. The lochs and glens, and wilds of Scotland came to mind.

Distance in Australia had to be a different animal.

From west coast to east coast, you could fit in the entire 48 lower states of the US, so Americans would understand. For Europeans, anything over an hour or even two is a hike. Locals consider that to be a drive, but not an untypical one. In his 1967 book, A Tyranny of Distance, Geoffrey Blainey references the reoccurring theme of distance in Australia. It's not just the distance between Australia and Europe, or the spaces between the State Capitals, but the way Australia lounged so far away from Britain.

The cars flitting past reminded me of the US. Six or eight-cylinder engines in a family sedan (saloon) car were typical. It was true Aussies chose mostly Ford or Holden. I was sure I'd seen the Holden Commodore as the Vauxhall Omega in the UK. Older Falcons were akin to the Ford Granada police cars I'd seen as a boy in the 1980s. Look under the bonnet and you will find a whopping 4,000cc engine. They seemed crazy big. *Built for local conditions* the marketing slogan rang.

Australians were proud of their car industry which created jobs politicians and workers appreciated alike, propped up by government subsidies. Locals paid over the odds for BMW and Mercedes. Cars were designed in Australia with an onshore build, for a local market—for long distances and dirt-roads. These cars handled corrugations to a homestead beyond the "Back of Bourke" as well as the winding Princes highway I took.

***

I noted a sign as I flew past.

> *Only a few k over*
> *You bloody idiot*

"Watch out for the cops," my cousin said. "They have zero tolerance down there."

It wasn't the only bleak sign on the roadside aimed at shocking motorists. I could expect to be pulled over if I was caught speeding. I glimpsed highway patrol cars in gaps of vegetation on the central meridian, radar guns at the ready. Sometimes a pursuit car was positioned ready to take off, or one was up the road in radio contact to flag a motorist down.

Cheap fuel was one thing, but the speed limit was another. It was a meagre 100 kilometres per hour, which was 60 miles per hour. In the UK I passed cops at 80 mph without them batting an eyelid, and it was the *autoroute* limit in France. But fair play—the Northern Territory didn't have a speed limit, and you could drive like Mel Gibson in *Mad Max*. Far out.

At Bega, the countryside inland formed part of the Southern Highlands—the sort of place where retirees with plenty of time on their hands bought large blocks of land, built self-indulgent homesteads out of local stone and laid out manicured gardens. There's a bit of money out this way, and I guessed you'd gauge this by stepping across the threshold of the local *Op Shop* and picking through cast-offs. (That's a charity shop for Brits—it's a fair name as everyone likes an opportunity.)

At the border, I stopped at a sign which had a cheerful, glossy montage of the best sights Victoria offered. The Great Ocean Road and the wine-making paradise of the Yarra Valley enjoyed high-billing. I squinted from behind my sunglasses and only saw fields. In Sydney, the vegetation presented as shiny or with a satin lustre; here further south, stark eucalyptus trees, scrub and dry grass dominated. I felt cars rush by with a draught, and it felt good to stretch my legs.

My relaxed demeanour soon turned to alarm when I noticed a splash of water on the tarmac between the front tyres. A small trickle followed the grooves and undulations of the hard shoulder. I traced it to the underside of the engine bay. My first worry was the coolant, but the splash ran clear, not green, and the reservoir looked topped-up. I carried on, keeping an eye out for the next repair shop, eyeing the engine temperature gauge for any telltale spike.

A mechanic's yard came up in a small town and I came to a halt in a dust cloud and a crunch of gravel. A bored apprentice in blue overalls and greasy hands greeted me. I showed him the drips.

"Air conditioning overflow, mate," he said. "All normal."

I carried on my way. When I felt tired, I simply pulled over at the side of the road for the night as the evening turned to dusk. It seemed convenient.

CHAPTER 8 MEXICANS

I found myself in a different state, but nothing changed, only the fact the car registration plates changed from yellow to white. The plate slogans: "Victoria—the Place to Be" so I knew at least I was now in the choice spot.

Squinting at cars as they approached, I noticed older slogans: "Victoria—On the Move" which had nothing to do with the fact minor earthquakes occurred out in this corner of the world. (They registered when a wall fell down somewhere in Melbourne.)

Studying plates gormlessly didn't hold my attention for long, and I amused myself by turning my attention to the sheep and cattle in the paddocks as I cruised on. "What About Me" by Shannon Noll played on the stereo.

The coast swung more westerly, and I headed for a well-known holiday destination—the Gippsland Lakes, halfway to Melbourne, where many Victorians spent their summer holidays, and I drove at the height of them. I passed through smaller places like Cann River, Bemm River, and Marlow; about the furthest Melbournians would drive.

Lakes Entrance looked like a frontrunner as a holiday destination, on the eastern side of a horseshoe bay. This sat opposite a narrow littoral of coast which ran straight as a light sabre for miles.

I took a break at Lake's Entrance, not wanting to stop long, as it heaved with New Year's tourists. I felt glad of an iced-coffee at a café and people-watched for a while. The foot-traffic consisted of holidaying families in singlets, thongs, long shorts and baseball caps who sauntered along the pavement. Utes pulling trailers laden with boats passed by, many still leaking water after retrieval, leaving a trail of water down the road. I could see one such launching and recovery spot where men and women (but mostly men) queued to get on the water to fish. It felt warm and sticky, and the breeze off the coast didn't help.

The inland highway ran ruler-straight. Tantalisingly, it ran due south for a short while along Lake Wellington.

At Sale, the highway continued west towards Melbourne and would take me to Taralgon, the heart of the Latrobe Valley within a few hours of the state capital.

I saw green farmland, singed yellow by the mid-summer sun. Rusty barns and cattle yards sparkled in the sunshine, with the occasional lone homestead with cars parked outside. What on earth happened in the barns? I didn't spot anyone. Maybe locals were enjoying an illicit, raucous swingers' party, but I wasn't invited.

The valley itself turned out industrial. It sited huge power generators which supplied Victoria and Melbourne with power. The generators belched smoke from high stacks. The brown coal burnt here is notoriously polluting and inefficient, and the Green parties in the State government tutted their dismay.

I found myself on a back highway when I took a wrong turn. It squeezed past a power facility near Moe, and large super-sized vat-shaped containers reached for the sky. I was just over ninety minutes from the outskirts of metro Melbourne and the highway continued relentlessly, but briskly, which I found encouraging.

I craned forward to read a sign.

Light Horse Museum

In the First World War, the Australian Light Horse military regiments recruited from this area. They would have been used in reconnaissance roles, or light skirmishing, as distinct from the heavy cavalry used by the British and French dragoons several centuries ago. The movies *The Light Horsemen* and *Gallipoli* (also Mel Gibson) came to mind. Both depicted young men from farming communities who got to Melbourne to enlist in their thousands when war broke out. The war effort had much to gain and little to lose with those pragmatic rural men.

I liked the local place names on roadsigns: Warrigal, Maryknoll, Bunyip—what are they? My favourite, though, was Nar Nar Goon. If that wasn't a place from *Star Wars,* then I didn't know what was. (I was thinking *Tatooine* maybe.) I pushed through the town of Pakenham, the terminus for the suburban MetLink train from Melbourne. This was the south-east corner of the city, the end of the line.

I passed turnoffs for new housing estates behind *Colorbond* steel-fences. Developers were selling "house and land packages" from offices set up in show-homes. To me, most of the houses looked box-shaped and lego-like. Hardly a mile went by without a sign for a new development, or the picture of a local real estate agent. Agents appeared to be based on the American model; more show than what we see in the UK. Their blow-up photos resembled politicians.

At Berwick, I was just about there. A former country town, but now the heart of new suburbs eating up tracts of former farmland. In the centre, houses had been established for decades. They looked American: one-storied villas. In any one street, houses had been built in different styles with a variety of materials—metal or tile roofs: timber or brick walls. I didn't see the uniformity I'd seen in the US.

A roundabout on a rise above the town gave me a chance to take it all in. I sized up the main street, divided by a beautified parking area. I drove through just below the speed limit, as slow as I dared. Time enough to make out coffee shops and restaurants—I picked out Thai and Italian; a Westpac bank, and a news agency. Patrons lounged at cafes under umbrellas, sipping hot coffees and taking the first bites of tart or cake. A stone memorial at a crossroads continued the First World War theme.

The road swung up a hill. On one side, a sheer drop, and I glanced over to see a homestead with a milk-urn mailbox, and a name on a swinging plank, within a glade bordered by old trees. At a crossroads, I parked outside a house, the hustle and bustle replaced by quiet. Nothing but the song of bellbirds, but the hum of traffic in Berwick now distant.

I rang the doorbell of a villa set back from the cul-de-sac, and stepped back. Two teenagers rode bikes at the far end, looping in circles like an aerobatic display team.

"How are you, Steve?" said Jane, opening the door and smiling.

CHAPTER 9 OLD TOWN

Jane and her husband lived in a small village on the edge of the metropolitan area. The village slumbered under the warm Antipodean day. A *milk bar* (corner shop/newsagent) at a crossroads looked like it stocked newspapers and essentials. Next door, a primary school, closed for the holidays, a play area and monkey bars unattended. The houses here were one-storey, but over the crossroads, I could spot grander two-storey houses on manicured blocks with tidy driveways lined by agapanthus plants. It looked like an exclusive stockbroker enclave on the outskirts of a UK city.

I knew the couple from London, and they'd moved out the year before with their two children. I considered them trailblazers. I followed Jane inside.

"Cup of tea?" she asked, as we sat in her kitchen with a sunken living area looking out on to a pool. I took off my baseball cap and placed my sunglasses on the table.

"That'll be great," I replied.

She filled the kettle.

"We've got no mains water, here, Steve. It's good in a way."

A local company trucked water in, and the owner lived in the next street over. It cost more, but stopped people moving in too readily, and a natural resistance to developers moving into sub-divide the land.

"How do you find it here, then?" I asked.

"We like it," she replied. "It's lovely here. It's less manic here than in your Sydney."

"I see what you mean."

"And—it's less than an hour to town from here," she added.

That seemed doable, I thought.

Melbourne metro stretched 50 miles (80 km) across. Urban sprawl was a defining factor of Australian cities, like their

US counterparts. London's population was twice the size, yet squeezed into a smaller area.

The conversation moved on to house prices, that very Anglo-Saxon pastime. Jane told me I was looking at $350,000-400,000 for a bush block. A bush block was a house with shrubbery, trees, perhaps more than just a grass yard, or a concrete area. This looked better than Sydney already. She told me more about the area and regaled me of the boutique vineyards in hidden corners suggesting the Melbourne climate or weather was not as cold as the distractors made out it was.

She made me an offer: "Stay the night. I'll show you around tomorrow."

***

After school drop off, Jane and I had a stop for a coffee, and a glance in the local real estate agent's window. We cruised Berwick's side streets, and I looked at the houses and the *reserves* (parks). It all seemed so new and shiny; even the older parts.

"This part is Old Berwick," said Jane. "It's the old bit, what would have been a country town. Let's take a loop back."

North of Berwick, we motored along rural roads and the traffic flowed freely. Views opened out into lush, rolling paddocks with meadows and distant hills on a hazy horizon. It looked to be horse country, with agistment stables, some with arenas in post-and-rail.

I found it reminiscent of the Thames Valley—a warmer version of Oxfordshire. It might have stood in for a tidy rural corner in the south-east of England—then I squinted harder and fancied Tuscany also described it.

"It's all drying out now in the heat," Jane said. "But when we arrived in spring, it was verdant."

My observation from the highway had been accurate.

Back in the kitchen, Jane cracked open the *Melways* and pointed to the pages.

"We're here. To the east is Gippsland."

That was the rest of country Victoria—the dairy farmland I had passed through. North-east, we could climb across the hills and mountains of the Great Dividing Range mountains to New South Wales with the River Murray the border.

She continued. "North: the 'Hills'; I'll show you those later." She pointed to an area coloured green. "Past them, there's a wine region called the Yarra Valley."

As I had seen, south—the never-ending build of new suburbs heading to the back bay. The city burbs sprawled to the north-west.

"I'll show you the suburbs," she said, and we jumped in my ute.

I could see the suburbs of Melbourne were organised on a grid system. Principle roads ran east-west—the map showed the Burwood Highway, High Street, Whitehorse Road and Wellington Road. North-south running roads intersected these at lights everywhere—we got caught at a red a fair bit. It looked busy, like London, but with more space for parked cars, and thoughtful town planners had constructed wider roads.

"You can buy a house off a main road and it's quiet," she explained.

She asked me to turn into a little maze of streets away from the traffic. They were tranquil, with a mix of houses with well-tended front gardens. Young children with mothers played in reserves. I understood the benefit of living closer to the city for work, without trucks speeding past. It seemed sleepier than London, with the convenience dialled up a bit.

"Dandenong is just there," she explained. "It's like a second city."

I saw a hotch-potch of streets with a single high street full of Indian, Afghan, and middle eastern eateries.

Jane had the street directory *Melways* in her lap, and she passed on tidbits of local knowledge.

Returning along the Burwood Highway, I saw wall-to-wall, flat, Melbourne on either side, then views of the Dandenong

Mountains ahead which sat patiently on the horizon, dense unscalable bush on its shoulders.

"That's pretty," I said.

"Isn't it? Let's head up," Jane replied.

The road left the hills on our left shoulder. We sped along a back highway which ran through bush and farmland, with lakes, and green, murky *dams* (ponds) out the front of people's properties.

Melbourne sits on a bay in a natural bowl facing the Tasman Sea. I found it astonishing when it sunk in there was nothing between the Australian mainland's most southerly city and Antarctica. Well, apart from Tasmania—the "Apple Isle", which rather spoilt my observation. And Tasmania is not small, it is still at least a quarter of the size of the UK.

The weather is different in Melbourne to other parts of Victoria. Weather systems sit in the bowl and circle the bay as the day progresses. The bowl is the Dandenongs, the "Hills". They rise to Mount Dandenong, at 400 metres above sea level, complete with TV antenna and car park.

Jane and I drove up, and I peered around with the keenness of a tourist. The terrain looked steep, and heavily forested in parts with colossal gum trees called Mountain Ash. The edges running along escarpments granted views, but you were really in the thick of it in places. Light struggled to filter through, and people built houses in tight corners on the hillside. It had a primordial feel.

Roads switchbacked and hugged the corners, and it looked easy to go the wrong way and end up in the wrong village. In storms, trees came down onto roads and houses. In 1997, fire tore through the ranges and caused damage.

The road passed through little picturesque villages such as Sassafrass, where I could avail myself of a stroll through a gift shop, look at a toy emporium, or enjoy a Devonish tea. The village of Olinda lay much further up "the mountain", and I grabbed a hot steak and pepper pie. On the way down, we took a side road past a rather kitsch restaurant called The Cuckoo.

"Have you heard of Puffing Billy?" she asked.

"Rings a bell," I replied.

It was world famous, in fact. The little train trundled the lower villages departing the town of Emerald which had a lake people used to cool down in summer. I first saw the train in a "Locomotives of the World"-type book as a boy in primary school. A serious-looking steam engine pulled period carriages full of shrieking primary school-age children from one side of the Hills to the other.

We slipped through another village across the valley. We ran past a timber Anglican church and a parade of shops on a shaded, enchanting tree-lined road. A fire station and milk bar stood across the road from a general store with wares for sale in wheelbarrows spilling on to the pavement. A sign boasted "$2.99 Ice!"

"If you want a rural idyll, I reckon you'll like this place," she said. "We looked here when we arrived."

It looked promising. I'd show Kiki when she arrived and knew she'd love it.

***

Lounging on the sofa, as Jane and her husband helped with their children's homework, later that night, I figured it was all workable. Distance to the city, the price of housing—the lure of the countryside all around. Kiki had liked the idea of Melbourne all along, so I rang her to confirm our idea, my heart in my throat.

"Hi…," she answered.

"Hey…" I began.

I gave her a run-down on what I had found.

"We're moving to Melbourne, what do you think about that?"

Kiki sounded delighted. And if *she* was, that made me happy.

CHAPTER 10 SHAKING OUT

So, Berwick was something old, and something new. It had one foot in established suburbia with new tracts of housing to the south and older villages to its north. I borrowed a *Melways,* and I lugged it everywhere.

I wanted to find a rental. I needn't look for a job immediately, so I had a few weeks of grace to focus on a place to live. I hoped the rental wasn't so hard to come about as I had the cash to stump up six-months' rent upfront, and references in hand, all part of my plan to schmooze a landlord's agent. I didn't want to spend an age traipsing backwards and forwards viewing houses.

Surely, the local branch of TJ Hooker had the answer? Peering at the listings in the window, I found a three-bedroom house advertised within walking distance of the town centre. I knew Kiki didn't have a current driver's licence and would need to be central to get organised when she arrived. The agent drove me there for a look.

He showed me a 1970s brick veneer house in a quiet side street, with a pink-hued gum tree in the front yard and recently cut grass. It had one living area which overflowed into a tiny kitchen, and three bedrooms and a bathroom. It had a good-sized back yard, with neat warm-weather couch grass, and a traditional "Hills Hoist" washing line. You could grab a handle and wind the laundry into a breeze.

"How much did you say it was?" I asked the agent who was dressed in a sharp suit and pointy shoes.

"900 bucks a month," he replied.

This was the bottom end of the range I expected to pay. As it was basic for a family, it would be exactly what we needed.

"I'll take it."

Bingo.

I shifted my suitcases in, lugged a mattress my friend had been about to throw out into the master bedroom, and parked out front. After living in apartments, I found it a novelty to have a back yard. I pegged my washing on the washing line, and from the kitchen window, watched it twirl in the breeze.

For groceries, I could walk to an independent chain called IGA. Invariably, I drove. I had good reason to: the local *bottle-shop* drive-in was one. A *bottle-o* was an off-licence (UK), or liquor store. Alcohol wasn't sold in supermarkets, unlike in the UK. It was satisfying to ask for a *slab* (carton) of say Coopers Pale Ale, from the convenience of your driver's seat and have it bought to the passenger side. If you didn't want *tinnies* (cans), there were *stubbies* (bottles). If I was undecided: the whole store side was open, so I could stroll in and take my time.

Speaking of the local supermarkets, I discovered a high-drama, high-stakes duopoly, a racket going on in the heart of Berwick. This was not the mafia in any normal sense, though. Two chains duelled for attention for shoppers: Woolworths and Coles. Between the two, they had sold fresh food and groceries to Australians for decades and the lack of competition meant you probably paid more.

Strolling down the aisle, with Jane, hands in pocket, I noted the absence of people walking barefoot. I had encountered people *sans* shoes (or in their pyjamas) with surprise in my backpacking year especially in subtropical New South and Queensland. I smiled at the goods that had seemed so quintessentially Australian in my first year.

One was Pavlova, a meringue-based dessert topped with cream and fruit—refreshing on a summer's day, sort of light and filling at the same time. It was a New Zealand invention. The story goes it had been served for a Russian ballet dancer earlier in the twentieth century. I reacquainted myself with Lamington, a cake with desiccated coconut flakes. It wasn't to all tastes.

"Oh look, Weetabix," I said, in the cereal aisle. "Only it's called Weet-bix here."

And as for the sweets you could buy in Woolworths in the UK:

"They are called *lollies*," Jane said.

In the UK you might say "ice cream lolly", but a lolly "Down Under" were sweets (and candy in the US). Another difference to confuse and confound. But independent grocers, butchers and greengrocers still did brisk business, and the range on offer seasonal. It had been a shame to see so many independents close in the British High Street.

"How ya goin'?" asked the girl on the checkout.

"I'm *good*, thanks." I remembered the line Australians favoured. The word "fine" was not required.

"Any plans for the afternoon?" she said.

Is she asking me on a date?

"Sorting out my rental, just moved to the area."

"That's great," she enthused.

My rental appeared to be a conversation killer. Clearly a date was off the table. I felt relieved that I didn't have to dust off flirting skills. Besides, she could multi-task: not only could she manage small talk, but packed my groceries too. In London, the disinterested assistant whizzed milk and bread to the bottom of the checkout, and I would have to overcome a rising panic and keep pace.

"How would you like to pay?" she asked, presently.

I paid cash. I liked the plastic money the ATM dispensed in cheerful colours. The polymer-coated notes lent a new meaning to the concept of money laundering. Anyone leaving a fifty-dollar note in a pocket, like I did, found it came out of the wash the same it went in. Each domination starting at five dollars from ten, twenty, thirty, fifty and one-hundred had a different colour: purple, blue, red, and yellow and green.

Living in Luxembourg with France and Germany so close, I had enjoyed seeking new treats. After slinging a bag of groceries on the counter one Saturday, I hung my washing and treated myself to a new one—a "Tim Tam explosion". Tims Tams were found in the chocolate aisle of Woolies. You dunked the caramel and chewy chocolate biscuit in coffee and popped it in your mouth before it disintegrated. The double chocolate ones were a *dead cert.*

It was good to see the choice in Berwick, but I was aware of where the real shopping took place, sort of US style.

"Just wait until you see Fountain Gate," Jane said. "It's a huge mall down the road towards Melbourne. It's fifteen minutes drive."

Looking to see for myself, I drove to Westfield Fountain Gate. I read Westfield Chadstone headed a league table of the largest malls in the southern hemisphere, if not Melbourne.

When I first laid eyes on Fountain Gate, I remembered the American malls I had seen in the 1990s. A labyrinth of corridors and halls housed K-Mart, Target, Best for Less and Big W. In K-Mart, I could buy fishing rods and tackle boxes, pillowcases, bedside-table lights, toasters and cutlery. (I didn't.) But I bought a *doona*, a quilt for my bed, and felt mightily pleased.

With sojourns back and forth, I appointed my living room with a TV, and speakers that could bust your eardrums. A plasma was outside my budget, so I chose a singularly large TV, (delivery promised next day). Call it a chance to make "boys" choices before Kiki arrived. Practical matters: I borrowed a fridge, and I got a secondhand Bosch front-loader washing machine from friends of Jane's—and cutlery and plates from Best For Less. I was "*baching*" it up, as they said here. I was the bachelor.

***

One evening after night had fallen, I was driving along the M1 Monash highway out-of-town back to Berwick. A sedan overtook me, and I saw incandescent sparks on the road fly under its rear wheels. The driver had taken a drag on their cigarette, and I'd seen the butt discarded out of the window.

A flashing blue and red light in my rear-view mirror got my attention. Police had been tailing me unnoticed. I pulled over.

The policeman ducked his head into the ute and sniffed the air.

"Ah, not you then," he said.

I realised he sought the smoker.

"Ah, yes, the driver in front." I pointed down the highway. I was not the guilty party.

Not me guv'nor.

"He's in trouble. Cigarette butts cause fires," the policeman observed. His man had got away. It was not just a littering offence, but something far more sinister. He asked me for my licence, and I fished out my Western Australian licence and told him I had only recently arrived in Melbourne.

"OK, but get yourself a Victorian one," he advised. I was free to go.

In 2002, on the Perth roads, I had got behind the wheel of a ten-tonne truck with a ten-tonne load, just so that I could get a job in the mining industry. It had 13 complicated gears split between a low and high range. Getting anywhere took a fancy bit of double-declutching. My licence was a Heavy Rigid truck licence.

I guessed converting this to a Victorian one was a matter of paying a fee and doing the paperwork at VicRoads, the local vehicle registration and licencing agency. The girl behind the counter took a photo and tapped away at her computer.

"Does Victoria recognise my truck licence?" I asked.

I'm a truck driver you know.

"Yup, here's a truck licence," she said. I was glad I was spared the indignity of a truck test.

That New South Wales plate needed to be swapped to a Victorian one. As the purchase was recent, all I did was pay a fee.

"I need to inspect your VIN number," she said.

She needed to check I hadn't bodged a ute together out of two halves.

I pulled up in a bay as directed, and she popped out of a door, mirror on a rod in hand. I thumbed the bonnet release. The VIN number married with the paperwork. She handed me the plates, and I affixed these with a screwdriver she passed over. Brighter people used cable ties to do the same job and were on their way in minutes.

CHAPTER 11 ON THE JOB FRONT

It was time to look for a job.

In my first year in Australia, I toyed with the grand notion of not working in IT again. I didn't miss the hours, the office locations, or the work. But I conceded as an engaged man with the inkling kids could be on the way in years, I had no option but to earn the big bucks.

"What's your name, mate? Steve? Good to see you."

I'd got talking to a winger in a rugby club, who worked in security. The club lay near Dandenong, and training was on Tuesdays. I found the *oval* (pitch) hard and dry. The team was full of large, well-built Pacific Islanders who could hit hard in the tackle. I was a bit older, and I wasn't sure how my body would cope. Still, I saw it as a chance to network.

He offered me the chance to sign up to get a security licence, on the chance I might need to get casual work. He directed me to an address in Dandenong and I showed up to find a bunch of rather serious-looking men with tattoos. City work was the go, though, and commuting by train an option.

A lot of corporates and companies headquarter themselves in Sydney or Melbourne. Out of the big four banks, two: ANZ, and NAB banks are headquartered in Melbourne. When I first arrived, people considered Sydney to have the edge in industries such as Finance, but generally, industries are split between the two. Given the opportunities in Melbourne, there was no real competitive advantage to being in Sydney. Salaries were on par, too.

The city didn't sprawl from nothing and had been planned. It centres on the Hoddle Grid, a rectangular grid of streets aligned south of west-east. Many Melbourne workers get office work in the vertigo-inducing tall towers where scores of medium to large companies locate their staff.

I was intrigued when I got the Metlink train into the city to see a recruitment agent sited on Elizabeth Street. The train from the south-east was an older train from stock, with soft foam seats covered in a coarse fabric which compressed rather too readily, and my back ached long before we reached the city. The train halted at stops on the way, and I resigned myself to the long haul. I got chatting to a middle-aged woman who explained which city loop station I needed to alight at for the city street I needed. She recited to herself, "King William, Queen Elizabeth," and pointed to a little map in her diary.

Kings and Queens of England?

Yes, but sure enough, the north-south running streets were King Street, William Street, Queen and Elizabeth. They intersected the key west-east running Flinders Street, and Collins Street in the CBD grid.

"So, get out at Flinders Street station, and walk up Swanston," she told me.

Flinders Station was a landmark terminus built in the nineteenth century with an impressive façade. Steps dropped to a major intersection at Flinders Street and Swanston. I glanced at an array of clocks set into the façade. Opposite, I noted the pub Young and Jackson, where I had a drink or two when I first visited Melbourne in 2002 on a scorching 40-degree day. The corner is a photo opportunity and part of classic Melbourne. Back in the day, before mobile phones, your most sensible option to meet someone lay "under the clocks". I once bumped, into Sylvester McCoy who played Doctor Who in the 1980s TV show. He told me he visited town for a sci-fi convention, and I think he felt quite pleased I recognised him.

People waited at the lights to swarm across the intersection or to cross the tram tracks to have coffee at Federation Square opposite, a recently built civic square with glass and concrete structures built in the early 2000s, to mark the 100th year since Federation.

As I found myself early for my appointment, I stood on the Princes Bridge looking south across the Yarra River along St Kilda Road.

Opposite on Southbank, the Arts Centre loomed, home to Hamer Hall, a 2,500-seater venue. A metal spire soared 150 metres above the ground resembling the Eiffel Tower. Further along, the casino, operated by Crown. I got the impression it never lacked for custom and the State's coffers swelled accordingly. Looking up, I saw the skyline dominated by tower blocks and skyscrapers. A thoroughly modern city.

Here, St Kilda Road formed a boulevard with tram tracks down the middle with plane trees alongside. The nineteenth century edifice of Victoria Barracks housed men and women of the Australian Defence Force, and an egregious overspill of offices, home to many IT companies stretched to near the bay at St Kilda beach. A flight of stone steps down to the river led to the Melbourne Cricket Ground and Rod Laver Arena, which hosted the Australian Open. Thousands of people would turn up for that alone.

There were also offices half-way near Albert Park. Senior managers and their nominated underlings enjoyed Grand Prix racetrack views from the top, and provided they slapped on the sunscreen could watch the cars whizz around all day.

But I needed to be north on Swanston Street heading towards the tower block I needed on Collins Street.

I hit Collins Street, Melbourne's principal thoroughfare running east-west. At the east end of the grid, I could find Parliament House with the Treasury Gardens and Captain Cook's cottage behind set in immaculate, tended grounds. I knew the cottage to be barely big enough to swing a cat in.

I found a food court at the base of the tower and coffee, and I scanned the tenant board to confirm the agent was here. It didn't take three minutes to scoot to the floor I needed in a lift so smooth I hadn't realised we'd even left the ground.

"Good to see, you, Stephen," the agent said, greeting me at reception.

She led me into a meeting room with a view of the Yarra and the Crown Casino, and we chatted for 40 minutes. She is sure my top-flight Luxembourg banking experience will see me in good stead; and she seemed confident it was just a matter of time before I landed a role. She wished me "Good Luck" and showed me to the lift well.

As I ambled back along Collins Street, proceeding alongside suited workers, or against the contraflow of others, another thought came to me.

Marvellous Melbourne.

Melbourne came to world prominence in the 1850s during the Gold Rush when the precious metal turned up in the fields to the west. With money came the fortunes. Melbourne grew rapidly. By 1890, it could boast of being the second largest city in the British Empire with almost 500,000 people. (I imagined Melburnians pleased to be getting one over on Sydney). Later, Sydney surged ahead never to be caught. *Them's the breaks*, I thought.

I imagined wealthy men and women perambulating along Collins Street. I can picture men doffing their hats to women. They would have travelled back to fabulous houses out in the East for afternoon tea. Now I saw teenage girls in low-rise jeans with jewel-studded belts.

Locals knew the eastern end of Collins as the "Paris" end as it held all the ritzy boutiques like Christian Dior and Gucci. There's also RM Williams, the well-known Australian bootmaker and outfitter. It felt less glam at the west end near Southern Cross station which accepted and discharged men and women in suits.

Speaking of suits, I thought I might need one, so I popped into a suit maker just off Little Collins Street. The fabrics were lighter, as befitted a hotter climate. I saw no need for the 14oz weight of my London West End suits. There's less need for a chalk-stripe here, too, so that's one suit from my older IT Finance days I could retire.

***

One day at home, I got a phone call from an agent who seemed to know all about me.

"Steve Malins…" he drawled by way of introduction. "How are you?"

"I'm alright, mate," I replied, my interest piqued.

He told me he was ex-military, and seemed to have taken a liking to me, I could tell. What's more, he'd found a job for me, a good fit too, and skipped to the important stuff—where the interview was, and a day he hoped I could do. I couldn't turn it down, and we finalised it there and then.

"You'll be fine," he said, and sent me on my way with his blessing.

I attended the interview in a north inner-city suburb, one only, and I felt relieved they didn't plan to put me through the wringer. Two seniors interviewed me, one an Englishman, who seemed friendly.

The co-director of the company came in as we finished with small talk. "Ah, I can see you are personable, that's great."

He sat down opposite. Perhaps he needed a break from his work. He made all the right noises. I figured at this point I'd got the job; hiring companies like people who can get along.

"The rate is fifty dollars an hour. You can invoice weekly," he told me.

That's $100,000 a year, not bad for a first job when the median wage was about $70,000.

He handed me a form. "Have you got an ATN?" he asked.

He explained the Australian Tax Number, which people received from any CentreLink office which handled tax, social security (benefits), and Medicare. I already had one from my backpacking days.

On the form I declared to the Australian Tax Office (ATO) this was my only income. As tax was inevitable, I paid it on my income in stepped brackets, but hurrah—the first $18,000 turned out to be tax free.

"You've missed most of the tax year, but you'll get tax back next year," he said, winking at me.

CHAPTER 12 MEN AT WORK

The company based itself on a smoke-filled first floor of a warehouse in Carlton, and I knew it would be a fun role with a good bunch of people. I tracked the smoke to an ash tray on a director's desk, who liked to pull on a cigarette and didn't appreciate anyone telling him to stub it out.

I drove in, finding a rat-run through the inner suburbs along Auburn Road to avoid getting stuck behind a tram on Glenferrie Road. I never tired of the cafes and boutiques of the inner east. If one particular set of lights had turned red, I liked to peer in the windows of an antique shop which had a flaking cement veneer in an attractive peach pastel, and white-framed architraves. But always, coffee shops.

It was in those early days back in the workforce that I came to be acquainted and understand the coffee culture in Australia, which is a phenomenon through all states and jurisdictions. I had grown up on English tea, breakfast or Earl Grey. Melbournians and Sydneysiders like their coffee and take it early, and several times during the morning or day.

It's part of the Italian heritage and not just anyone will operate the gleaming *espresso* machine. A qualified barista will have done a course. Patrons form a relationship with an owner and place their trust in their teenage barista. If they don't do a good job, then the savvy customer won't return and tell their friends. We had no need for chains such as the US Starbucks or the UK Costa in a market saturated by independents. Few Melbournians will drink their coffee black, in a shot; most will have milk with theirs in a *latte* or a flat white. I had never even heard of these when living in London and asked for a *cappuccino*. Some asked for double shots, and got a stronger caffeine fix, rather than return later.

The bloke next to me had *three* morning coffees, and retreated to the loo, with the *Herald Sun*—where he ran down the clock.

I loved seeing the way Melbournians walked their dogs or fetched the newspaper, wearing baseball caps and sunnies before work. They saw it as a daily ritual. They met friends for a first coffee before heading to the shower and a change and jump on a tram to get to work. And if they were busy, they would transport their drink in a takeaway paper cup, on the go, in small, medium or large as if it were gold.

I saw how women dressed for the climate, often in thongs—at odds with their business dress. Maybe they had shoes under the table at work and changed once they had ascended the lifts in their tower block.

I enjoyed the fun lunches we had on Fridays. We enjoyed a bottle of wine with our meal in the local pub down the street, taking turns to order another bottle, then another. On the warmer days we snagged a table in the beer garden, with the heat of the day rising, the UV smashing the back of your neck once the sunlight moved over.

"The only rule in the office is if you have a drink you don't return to work," said a director, taking a sip from a well-filled glass.

So, with this pronouncement, he had placed us on notice, but we took due notice of his red, stained lips. He chuckled one day to see one of our contractors locking his Porsche.

"We pay these guys too much money," he lamented.

We enjoyed shorter lunch trips to Victoria Parade in East Melbourne, and the Vietnamese food. Coming from a city where Indian cuisine ruled supreme, like Vindaloo, or a Korma, I loved trying other Asian cuisines. My favourite had to be fried beef or chicken presented on a bed of rice, which arrived sizzling on an earthenware dish. (The waiter used a cloth to shield his hands from three-degree burns.) We added chilli flakes from condiment trays or laced the rice with hotter yet chilli oil.

Sydneysiders and Melbournians handle Asian food with ease

in a way we hadn't seen growing up in Europe. I noted my colleagues were familiar with chopsticks and handled them with aplomb, (I refused to be self-conscious about the fact I struggled with mine).

The lunch hour flew by too soon, but sometimes we saw the laid-on entertainment of a drug deal outside in the street. Occasionally a plains-clothes member of Victoria police would swoop from an unmarked car and take the dealer and buyer into custody.

"There goes another bust," one of my colleagues, a Tasmanian, would say in his slow tones.

I had a sneak at the newspapers, figuring I needed to get up to date with current affairs. There didn't seem that many to choose from.

I had got used to the variety of the UK press. Shops sold the red mast-headed tabloids *The Sun* and *The Mirror,* the main "rags". If I needed my daily dose of sleaze and gossip, I could rely on these. We had no such thing as a "Page Three girl" Down Under. The "quality newspapers" had been the broadsheet *The Times* and *The Independent.*

Here, I found Victoria's *Herald Sun*, the tabloid, and *The Age*, the highbrow newspaper. Also, *The Australian,* which claimed to be the national broadsheet but had a bit of a Sydney-bias.

The Age had a left-wing slant. It was owned by Fairfax Media, who printed the sister paper *The Sydney Morning Herald.* It was the paper of choice for the inner-city left-voting dweller. I thumbed through *The Australian* one lunchtime. It covered the east coast Rugby, and I liked the national aspect of it. It was the Murdoch-owned "right-wing" paper, but I noted in good conscience it had a perfectly good Arts section.

We had a bumper weekend paper on Saturday, and feet up, over coffee, I luxuriated in the back yard with *The Weekend Australian* or *Saturday Age*. Both came with a magazine and a current affairs pull-out. The UK press had run a big newspaper on a Sunday for as long as I could remember. In Melbourne, the more substantial paper came out on a Saturday, and they saw fit to push out a more light-on edition on Sunday. *Vive la difference.*

CHAPTER 13 RECONCILIATION

I called home and gushed to Kiki things were going well and that I was earning. I felt grateful to have a job as a newly arrived migrant, and that I wasn't driving taxis around town, or standing outside a nightclub.

One Friday night, I had a drink with work colleagues. In the dark, I walked back briskly to the office to get my laptop. I pressed the button to open the roller door, ducked under it, and pressed it again to close the door behind me and galloped up the stairs to the office. After ten minutes, I ducked back under the shutter door. I heard a man shout: "Victoria Police!"

I froze in an instant and looked around.

No sudden move.

"Who are you," said a man. He wasn't in uniform, but obviously in plain clothes.

"I work here, mate."

"Where have you been?"

"Just in the pub. Around the corner."

"We had a report of a burglary near the pub. You say you work here?"

It turned out to be an misunderstanding: the policeman told me he had got a call from a local homeowner who had been burgled, had seen me and followed. He had thought me up to no good and got on to 000. It must have been my backpack and hurry. No harm done.

"OK buddy, good to go," said the cop.

"Thanks." I made sure to be understanding whatever the circumstances. As a new migrant I didn't fancy being evicted from Australia so soon.

***

Kiki had meanwhile progressed the sale of her flat in south

London and had sold her furniture. She busied herself packing and getting organised, just like I had. She squeezed a few things into boxes for shipment but let a treasured kitchen table go. Some migrants filled an entire 40-foot shipping container—I had heard prices in the area of £9,000—or shared one to save costs. I could imagine the much-loved contents of a home on the High Seas going via the Suez Canal or around the tip of South Africa.

I couldn't wait to get to the airport. It was going to be the first day of the rest of our lives together. The evening before, I swept, dusted, and vacuumed the bedroom. I brought the sheets in off the line and made the bed. The drive took an hour, and I felt nervous. We were reunited in the arrivals' hall. My heart performed backflips as Kiki pulled her luggage though the customs door, and we embraced.

"Baby, great to see you," she said.

We embraced. It felt good to see her, but even better to feel her. She glanced down and admired my new boots.

"What are they?" she asked.

"RM Williams," I replied, thrusting a foot forward.

These were a legend of Australia, a best-known brand. They shod everyone from a farmer at a Bachelor & Spinster ball to a Prime Minister at Kirribilli House. I had chosen a smart Chelsea boot in brown calfskin, with a squared-off chisel toe. The upper had a one-piece construction, and the leather as smooth as a baby's bottom. They had run tight for the first week or so, but were just about broken in.

"Four-hundred bucks!" I claimed.

"I want a pair too," she retorted.

I hoisted her bags onto a trolley, and I steered it out to the car park. Our first port of call was a bedding store. We needed a new mattress, and I wanted her to choose. We took back roads home. I wanted to show her the countryside and tracts of paddocks and views of the Dandenongs. We didn't need to jump on the M1 Monash highway and flit along in the greyness of the suburbs—it was time to show off.

"It reminds me of Mexico," she said, gazing around.

I relaxed a bit. It was great to see her after a few months apart, and we exchanged little happy glances as I drove us back home.

I introduced her to our house, showed her the kitchen and what I'd got to tide us over until we could replace it with better stuff. I introduced her, triumphantly, to the whizz-bang Bosch washing machine and murmured "Fifty bucks." She ducked her head in the bedrooms, and I explained I hadn't even gone into them—all the less to clean. She nodded, and agreed it would suit us until we found a place of our own.

"Like the *doona*?" I asked, eyebrow raised. "The quilt, I mean?"

"I love it!" she said.

She spent time prettying the house, and introducing, perhaps, a woman's touch. A vase of flowers placed on the mantelpiece transformed the area. We never touched *Bedroom Two* or *Three*, and they became shrines to whoever had last cleaned them. When I returned from work the next evening, a superior set of sharp knives sat on the kitchen counter replacing the set I had been hacking away with. Kiki had cooked supper for us both and I tucked in glad to be relieved of kitchen duties. It felt special to enjoy those moments together.

CHAPTER 14 STERLING WORK

The wine bar on Collins Street looked like it would do. Kiki had a glass of wine; I had a *schooner* (three-quarter pint) of Carlton Cold beer. We chinked our glasses. She could see how the Hoddle grid worked—this was it; this was *town*. Passing Flinders Street station, we walked over the bridge and looked out across the Yarra River. The lights of cafes and residential skyscrapers casted pink, blue and orange light into the night sky. Evening diners walked across the footbridge and veered off towards the Casino. Down there, we spotted flames erupting out of installations on the pavement outside the foyer. We felt an autumn chill in the air, but Kiki looked around excitedly at her new city with a smile.

It had been a while since I had the simple, but good, food I had found in France. We jumped on a tram which trawled south down St Kilda Road and took a left at Domain junction. We found a little bistro on Toorak Road near South Yarra train station called France Soir. It sold itself as being the sort of place you'd find in an unknown French town, off the autoroute perhaps. I didn't think it was wide of the mark.

We found the floor crowded of an evening, with diners almost elbowing each other, and waiters squeezed between the square-checked tablecloths of the tables adopted the right level of surliness and contempt.

Kiki had French Onion soup. I started with a tray of *escargot*, each poor little snail swimming in its own butter, but conceded that with the amount they used I might as well be eating chicken. Steak and chips with pepper sauce brought back those long two-hour Luxembourg lunches. Kiki had a vegetarian option. The *crème brûlée* cracked perfectly with the back of a dessert spoon, and all I had to do was savour every mouthful and roll my eyes.

***

The southern autumn set in at the end of April. I was convinced someone had flipped a switch. In May, the stable warm, even hot, days of March—already cooling in April, were replaced with cold starts and skies that were often overcast. By winter, those grey skies would be the norm. This wasn't Sydney.

As in a northern autumn, leaves fell off the trees, only it was the non-native deciduous species that left an ornamental collection on the pavement. The eucalypts remained intact, so the residual green staved off the stark, colourless canvas of a European winter.

The colder days weren't stopping us from getting on with things. I wanted to show Kiki the houses we could buy. We pondered the house that would meet our needs.

In London, the first thing an Australian noticed when going to their digs for their first night—in Shepherd's Bush (later Notting Hill)—probably in a shared house with other Antipodean friends, is that the houses were *tiny*. Millions of Brits live in terraced housing, or in semi-detached houses. But we didn't want to buy a house joined in a row with others, or a house divided into two.

A semi-detached house in London had a hallway leading to a kitchen at the other end. We'd have a living room—a "sitting room", or "lounge", and a dining room. We'd be lucky to have a small garden, maybe a patio. We'd have two to three bedrooms, and there would be no *en suite*. If we owned a detached house, we'd be getting ahead of ourselves, and a Grade One heritage listed, house would have been the jackpot.

Compared to the space North Americans have, privacy might have been more of an issue in London, but Brits suggested walls were thick enough. I wasn't so sure—my downstairs neighbour in my old block reckoned he could punch his hand through his wall, which was saying as much about him as the engineering.

Australians live in townhouses and *units* (flats) too, but

suburbanites live in detached houses on a block with a front and back *yard* (garden). The traditional *block* (plot, section in New Zealand) came in at a quarter of an acre—1,000 square metres. In recent years, developers have created new suburbs where buyers built large houses on smaller blocks of land—a *house and land package.*

A block of land to build on came in at typically 600 square metres. With progress, and developer's profits, blocks were getting smaller. By 2004, suburban Australians seemed to operate on the basis if they couldn't live near the city, or even grow veggies in their back yards, they could at least use their large house as a theme park.

"Have you seen the home theatres?" asked Kiki, looking at a brochure.

Just about every new house had one. Even the older houses were huge. Houses didn't just have two living areas, but potentially a third. I surmised the furniture chains such as Harvey Norman ("Hardly Normal") made a small fortune when homeowners bought several suites on interest-free credit to fill these spaces, even if they were never used.

***

So, we sold two flats in London, one each,
after the housing boom had raged for four years. We had no way of knowing whether we had sold at the top, or whether a crash might be around the corner. I had bought after the first London price spike—prices had been steadily rising since the late 1990s.

"Get into property," someone had said in a London pub in 1998, but that advice fell on deaf ears. "Now's the time to buy," he implored.

I figured as a real-estate agent they were talking up the market. I turned out wrong, and with hindsight, I bought later than I would have liked. Still, we were both sitting on equity. It was a classic London dinner party conversation, of course, and had been for ages. People loved talking about how much their houses were worth. But as one bloke at work said,

"But you buy and sell in the same market." He tried to be prosaic about the whole madness. "What would you do with the cash if you sold, anyway? Are you going to live in a box?"

Well, we weren't—we wanted to use that equity to buy in a market where we got about 2.5 dollars to the pound which boosted our chances of owning a house with land somewhere.

This was not France, where we could buy a chateau or old water mill on a sprawling estate for next to nothing. Australia was not cheap—we had missed the boat there, reflecting the fact it had to be a prime destination of choice for people all over the world. The advice seemed you got more for your money and avoided the lifestyle conundrums of London.

Spending pounds took the sting out of purchases. Some Brits moved to Australia and loaded up with new cars, jet skis and all sorts of clobber in a sort of one-shot of extravagance. A mate had moved to Australia in 2001, and we dined together one Sydney winter's evening in 2002. In a plush restaurant off George Street, he recounted how he had exchanged three dollars to the pound and had bought the house of his dreams. This wasn't so far-fetched when during my travel in 2002, I often got 2.7.

"Steve. That housing cash. When are you going to transfer the money over?" Kiki asked me.

I looked at her feet, at the custom-made black RM Williams that enclosed them. She had plumped for a pointed toe and a Cuban heel. We had popped into the Collins Street shop at the Paris End for her to order them, and I had bought a pair of moleskin trousers which made me look like Tom Burlinson from the movie *The Man from Snowy River*.

"I'll get on to the transfer," I replied.

We had set up an Australian dollar account with a company specialising in holding your pounds and advising you when to exchange. The pound headed down, and so a young rep advised me to set my lower limit, hoping it might recover. We hit the backstop, and my British pounds converted that night into dollars, at 2.4, and she rang me in the morning to tell me. I imagined the smirk of the computer as it pushed the button for me overnight.

If it had any Artificial Intelligence, maybe it worked out the money I had lost over a year might have stretched to a new car. Instead, that car came in the form of a second-hand Ford sedan. It was a large, fast and comfortable car, and Kiki passed a driving test after a few refreshers.

But that cash burnt a hole in our pocket.

CHAPTER 15 LOOKING FOR
THE AUSTRALIA DREAM

For our "forever" home, we looked at the glossy weekend property pull-out section in the Saturday newspapers and kept a lookout in the estate agent windows. Friends rang up to tip us about houses they had seen.

We both had the romantic notion we wanted a detached house on a bush block and the villages we saw seemed to fulfill our rural/urban dream. Kiki even liked the idea of chickens and a veggie patch. For a country famous for agriculture and large farms, *stations,* many Australians in the main live in suburbs in the capital cities.

You couldn't turn on the TV in the UK without seeing people moving to the sun. The agents repeated their annoying mantra: "Location, Location, Location."

I asked at work, to find the hot suburbs and the places people were interested in. I gave a colleague a lift home one afternoon, and he explained it all.

Melbourne traditionally had sprawled to the east. The wealthy who built established homes in the inner East—in places like Toorak and Kew wanted to arrive in the city and leave the city with the sun behind them, not in their eyes.

At eight o'clock in the morning, the West Gate bridge which connects the western suburbs to the docklands area saw bumper to bumper traffic. Despite the rush hour, everyone slowed, blinded by sunshine.

Lots of people, including families, lived right in the city centre. There were plenty of residential high rises to choose from, and it must have been convenient being right in town near work. The edges of the city, recent beneficiaries of gentrification called; Port Melbourne, South Melbourne and Middle Park.

The Bayside areas reminded me of Sydney, with people

enjoying the sands or esplanade, morning or evening. The north side of Melbourne housed a cosmopolitan crowd in places such as Carlton and Fitzroy—I heard people refer to them as the "pink end" of town. They were full of interesting and colourful housing stock large enough to bring up a family. Federation homes, built around 1901 when the States incorporated, looked good. They were timber homes on narrow frontages in archaic cobbled streets.

The east housed the prime real residential estate. If the north lay claim to be the place of the trendy, then the east claimed established territory—the tree-lined avenues in the adman's lingo. Toorak Village on Toorak Road was swanky and gave rise to the term "Toorak Tractor", a large 4x4 SUV. True piles and mansions owned by influential people and celebrities cost a pretty penny. People liked the Californian Bungalow with brick pillars supporting a front porch and a gabled eave. Many places were served by the tram network.

Trams felt a superior way of getting around. They were heavy, and clunked noisily down the street tailed by cars. I loved hopping on one with a book, looking up to see the cafes and houses roll past. They emptied and sped up in the suburbs, like a light rail. The tram stopped frequently with a whoosh of opening doors. Cars following on behind were required to stop to the rear at once, flagged by warning lights and a siren. Once the tram doors closed, cars overtook either side like schools of fish darting past a shark. Whilst new trams had wheelchair access, antiquated trams lacked air conditioning and on 37-degree February days, people melted like a soft-serve ice cream.

I dropped my colleague off in the middle suburbs in the east; established heartland. The middle suburbs started past the north-south running Warrigal Road. This is precisely where you would position a family of average means, the sort of family fit for a TV show. I might have been thinking of the *Neighbours* show my school mates had been glued to in the 1980s. I leaned forward to read the name of a nearby court, or cul-de-sac.

Pinoak court

In this court, I found the house as used in the exterior shots of the show; and it was *as per the house* I saw on the TV as a child. Few people were around, and I suspected only annoying British people of a certain age—like me— stopped to gawp. The house infact looked like a typical villa made from *brick veneer.*

It was a simple method of construction. They framed up out of pine on a concrete slab or stumps. The roof—also timber, either prefabricated tresses or a traditional ridge roof. The brick walls did not hold up the roof—hence the term.

Looking up and down the road, no homeowner accosted me, nor does the dog Bouncer come rushing out for a pat. I didn't spot "Mrs Mangel", or "Madge" either. I headed back home pleased that whilst I had lost a precious half-hour of my life, I could say I'd been.

The middle suburbs gave way to the foothills of the Dandenongs such as places evocatively named Ferntree Gully, or semi-rural pockets such as Warrandyte. I saw a place on the map called Kangaroo Ground, and further out, Diamond Creek. *Whatever happened there?* I wondered.

Finally, there were the outer burbs: "the burbs". They had a bit of a reputation.

"Nothing ever happens there," one colleague lamented at lunch. "It's dead."

It looked as if he had grown up in an outer suburb and stayed clear ever since. He said they were for *bogans.*

"Bogans?" I asked.

"A name for people with little class or taste," he said.

There was a lot written about them in popular culture. A bogan song might be the Australian classic "Khe Sanh" by the 1970s band Cold Chisel, which united all Australians. There's a joke there's a bit of bogan in all Australians.

We didn't want to be cramped in the inner-city, nor could we afford the luxurious and splendour of the inner east, nor want the no-man's-land of the middle suburbs.

So, we came back to where we were. We looked around Berwick. We found a real mix, new houses and older houses in various need of renovation.

We decided a *house and land package* on a new estate was not for us, and there were plenty of these. I didn't want the problems of a new house, and developers were building on land that had been flood pains. Neither of us liked the idea of no trees. Sure, the ones planted would mature in 15 years, but I didn't think I could wait that long.

There'd be little or no shade, or respite, from the long, hot Melbourne summers. To squeeze houses in on smaller blocks, the houses had minimal eaves. Where was the shade? The roofs ended at the wall as if they had been built from Lego.

Kiki said, "Do you realise? People living there would need to run air conditioning all summer."

"It's a fair point," I replied.

We saw a rather listless feel to these new estates. Not only did they remind me of a "toy town", but they also had a "Stepford Housewives" feel. They were popular with a generation of Australians who had been brought up in older homes that wanted more space and lifestyle living, and less maintenance. It was courses for horses.

We noticed the traffic south of the main highway looked worse than the traffic north. The north contained the section known as "Old Berwick"; established avenues and side streets, and a few were the standouts; prime real estate. And north again, were the villages we admired, which seemed a happy medium between the rural life we wanted and the opportunity to be close enough to work in the city.

CHAPTER 16 BUYING AND $ELLING

"**H**ey Steve."

"How's it going mate," I replied, squinting into the sun.

It was my neighbour, a handsome man in his seventies, with a pleasant smile. He sidled up next to me, *Herald Sun* under his arm. Our gaze fell on the real estate agent suited and booted out the front of a house a few doors down. We were at an unlikely looking single bedroom house for sale. None of us had the slightest interest in buying, we were fellow "*sticky beaks*"—nosy people, in cahoots together.

Auctions were popular in Australia. Vendors chose to go to auction for highly desirable properties. Buyers paid a fair bit more than they would offer to secure their dream home when the pink mist came down, but they risked getting sucked into a standoff.

On the day, tens of people turned up to bid, morning coffee in hand. The bidding started at a likely amount. If no one bidded, the agent put in the seller's "own bid", announced somewhat smugly. Bidding followed in steps of say $10,000.

This was fascinating to watch, and it only took a nod from an interested party, or a wave of a rolled-up prospectus to take the bidding up in increments towards the price the seller hanged out for. I will spare you the story of the man who inadvertently acquired a new house when all he did was swat a fly.

Trust me when I say you can treat auctions as a morning out you can squeeze in after fetching *The Age*. For others, it depended on whether it could be squeezed in before Tarquin needed to be at ballet. My neighbour and I were no different.

We stood respectfully near the back and watched. I'd heard of auctions where no one bidded at all. This was one of those. The auction "passed in" with no offer. But we wanted to buy the way we felt comfortable: by offer.

CHAPTER 17 GRAND TOUR

Like a criminal who returns to the scene of the crime, our interest came back to the village I had driven through, across the valley from where I had stayed.

We'd seen places for sale advertised in the local estate agent's window, so on a Saturday, we grabbed the weekly newsletter from the agents in Berwick. We drove up the hill to the township at a crossroads.

As diligent home buyers, our eyes flitted across the amenities. We noted a supermarket with jacked-up prices, a post office, bakery, hardware store, a milk bar, steak restaurant, and chemist. All the essentials. The hardware store had a dirt lot to the side with divided sections selling gravel; various grades, feed for horses, firewood and mulch. It all felt promising out of the box. A road we liked the look of from the map was a left turn here.

Kiki said, "I love the way we could just turn without having to drive anymore. We'd enter the village—BANG, we're home."

"Let's see," I replied.

The road turned out to be a tree-lined avenue with established houses on both sides, a few hidden under eucalypts at end of driveways, others less shy, sitting square on their generous-sized blocks. Autumn leaves on the non-native trees were in full colour. I loved the flame-orange tints. A few leaves were green with a coiled edge in contrasting brown; others were yellow resigned to the shortening days. Others were a deep red, days away from falling to join others lying heaped and composting on the ground. It was nice either way.

After a kilometre, the road turned at right-angles. Just before the turn, three grand houses in prime position took our breath away. One was a tidy, white timber mansion, with two gated entrances and driveways leading to established manicured gardens, and tennis courts. It had a swish colonial vibe. Two mulberry trees, and a stark ornamental pear completed the grandeur.

But once past the turn, we gasped to see the tree canopy peter out, and the road open and descend into a vast valley. Our viewpoint from the top granted us commanding views to the hills and peaks of the Dandenongs straight ahead. Houses scattered the hillside, and we saw other little hamlets in the distance, smoke coming from chimneys. I saw tall conifers further down, but these were well below us. The colours and hues of the green hillside provided a patchwork effect, and the autumn sun that day created haze in pockets to draw the eye.

Yet again, I drew parallels with the gardens of England. We might be on the North Downs outside London, in prime commuter belt, or on the rolling escarpment of the South Downs of Kent further away. As it sank in later, we could well be in a southern department of France, even a corner of Italy.

Kiki thought the location a winner, and I had to agree. She had fallen in love with this back pocket.

We had to nip back across the village to a viewing before it closed. It was a four-bedroom house on a secondary, but choice route through the village, on a quarter of acre. Built in the 1970s, it had a triangular-shaped gable, common in those days, and had a high cathedral ceiling which seemed grand to a Londoner. Our eyes lit up at a huge living area and kitchen, and a glass wall to the backyard. Tilting our heads back, we saw the glass arched floor to ceiling. A strike against it: it had no *en suite* bathroom to master, which on reflection, seemed an oddity. This would be challenging presumably once the first of a whole young brood of Malins arrived. I did note, however, the local pub and bottle shop lay across the road.

And a bonus: the last two houses were in that fantastic little valley.

The second lay square in our budget, and make no mistake,

we noted houses in the village considerably more ambitious. It had three bedrooms. The master bedroom sat alongside the kitchen, and both looked out on to lightly wooded bush, about half an acre all up. The current owners were using the master as a light-filled studio which made the house. If we planned to grow a family, we would be required to press it into service as a bedroom.

We thought the living room, an area next to the kitchen cramped, a definite downside. The entrance was through an elevated area near the entrance and other bedrooms. The seller had placed a tiny pool table near the front door, but the raised area seemed a poor use of space. We questioned the utility.

We liked the opportunity the land gave us but didn't think the house quite suited us.

They had priced the next house at a cool $400,000. It wasn't a big house at all, but larger than our rental and within budget. The brochure advertised an entire acre of land which impressed us on the one hand. It was, in fact, a skinny acre with a narrow frontage, so the land stretched 200 metres to bush. Bush took one-third all up. Again, coming from London this smacked of pool winners' proportions. It lay on a section of dirt road as the tarmac road ended 100 metres further up, but this didn't worry us.

The front had a gravel driveway room for five cars, a front garden, with agapanthus, a common enough leafy perennial plant used to ornament driveways which flowered in lilac. It appeared priced to sell.

It presented as a simple one-storey "L"-shaped house with three bedrooms, one with *en suite*, and an area divided into kitchen (room for a table), living area (bookcases and a space to sit) and TV.

We gasped when we saw its selling point. A large deck at the rear of both living area and kitchen got our attention—and the entire back of the house opened onto it. It was the size of the living room and kitchen, and it practically doubled their size as a living area: we could spill out there in the warmer months. In winter, we could get those plastic strips cafes use, or a gas heater. A pergola provided a canopy against rain and sun.

There were views out across trees to a ridgeline in the distance, with properties perched on the horizon. The house next door was just visible on the boundary, and we looked down on its metal-roofed pergola that had ornate balusters and dusty pilasters. The back yard descended into an overgrown paddock and tree line.

"Look at the pool," Kiki said under her breath.

We saw an above ground pool with a deck all around. I guessed it at ten metres long and filthy, but it was not uncommon for people to let their pools go a bit in winter if they had busy lives. It ran the entire length of the back deck behind a railing. Access to the backyard was via a narrow flight of stone steps, and I imagined standing there on a mild evening or lounging on the deck in summer. The agent explained that unlike new kitchens, pools didn't increase the value of a home, but they might increase the likelihood of a sale.

Right.

Another bonus: the kitchen had not long been installed, and we admired the timeless style. Sort of French Provincial kitchen: white timber with chamfered edges and grooves running vertically, and a dark surface, not granite (which became fashionable later), but adequate for our needs. Kiki reckoned many fads came and went and dated houses; this kitchen would serve us for many years.

The floorboards were pine, soft, and not as sought after as the luxury lighter-coloured Tasmanian Oak or dark Jarrah hardwood found in prestige houses, but cheery. I noted a firewood box accessible from outside. Reaching into the box from inside to ferry wood to the wood burner would be easy.

On the downside, we accepted it a bit run-down, and both the pergola and deck needed a coat of paint and a good oil.

We appreciated the wood burner, which I thought would be great during winter—"cave man" TV I suggested. I could see the definite appeal of sitting in front with a glass of wine. The current owners had the right idea and had artfully positioned a long chaise longue alongside. They had a country vibe going on, with tapestries, carpets, an old formal desk and bureau; and they had turned half of the "L"-shaped living area into a formal dining room with a polished table.

Tumbling back out the front, we noted empty paddocks across the road belonging to neighbours who lived opposite further down. Their house wedged in trees that ran to the horizon. It was tranquil, and we saw so much space.

Time to confer. I said, "So, which one did you like?"

"The last one," Kiki said.

"I thought the second one looked interesting with that studio, but not quite what we need," I replied. "But that deck and pergola on the last house was impressive."

She loved it: she considered this last one the pick of the bunch. The agent mentioned the area had an environmental significance overlay which meant we had to be careful what we did with the land. The rural location meant developers were unlikely to split the large blocks to build houses.

We drove the area which sprawled over about ten square kilometres. Livestock—cows and sheep grazed at larger properties, hobby farms maybe. We negotiated dirt tracks and pulled up at properties, sneaking a peek. We could get lost in any of the back roads that snaked around.

There were fascinating little corners and blocks with sleepy homesteads, more than a few with impressive wood piles stacked for winter. We saw goats roaming freely in one. A ram stood on a hill the owner had created with an excavator. The sure-footed animals loved to climb and would take any opportunity going.

***

We weren't sure about these houses when we viewed them, and

we saw them in winter when they weren't portrayed in the best of light. I got busy at work; leaving in the dark and coming home in the dark. I wondered if the village might be a bit too far from the city, just under fifteen minutes of extra driving which added up after a long day. We agreed, though, it *was* nice, and if we bought out here in the south-east, we would be back in the village ideally.

We had another look at the city, to see if we could change our minds on city-living. In the main, we weren't impressed. We didn't want an apartment in the city, and the small houses we saw in the east were grungier and prices were climbing.

Colleagues were buying out west in places such as Seddon and Footscray at the older docks. For years these had been seen as the poorer cousins for Melbournians, but as places gentrified, younger people moved there as they were priced out of the east and north. We had no plan to buy, then size-up later; we'd be stung for stamp duty. Our goal: to buy once and cry once.

We visited a colleague from work in such an archetypal weatherboard cottage. Often these were worker's cottages build in the nineteenth century. Characteristically long and skinny, they retained a heritage frontage. Typically, the owners had sanded a long corridor, taking it back to the original boards, the 1970s-1980s carpets long gone. The corridor ran the depth of the houses, with a parlour at the front, bedrooms along the side with a kitchen at the rear to a small backyard. We could see why they were well sought after.

We didn't see the point in buying in the middle suburbs; prices had climbed faster than we'd prefer, and it struck us we'd have none of the advantages of rural living, nor the amenity of the city. I conceded I would be closer to work, but that was the only upside I could see.

***

It sure wasn't getting any warmer, but we had a day when the sun burnt down in a cloudless sky and the mercury hit 19 degrees. One Sunday morning, we saw the third house we looked at advertised in the local paper. The line they had chosen for full effect was the "Affordable Acre."

"Look," Kiki said, handing me the newspaper. "The house we saw."

I noticed the tagline:

Room for a pony.

The Saturday newspapers carried swish supplements of houses on sale. The house wasn't special enough to grace these pages, but an editor saw it fit to include in the local press.

The price had dropped to a cool $375,000. We called the agent in the morning, and she remembered us. (I suspected she could sniff the first-time buyer from the UK.)

We asked to inspect the Section 32 which declares the easements or covenants attached to the property. An easement is a water pipe, phone line or sewer. We saw these as "special instructions" on the property. We noted the environmental overlay which protected the local flora and fauna.

Our first act: we offered $300,000, and the vendor declined. The vendor agreed on our next offer of $337,500, our second act. Maybe we were obvious in splitting the difference. But as the agent told me, we had bought the cheapest acre she had sold in years. The agent confided in me it was a good price. (The house had fetched $180,000 in the early 1990s.)

You make your money when you buy, not when you sell, is the old estate agent advice. We had bought the "cheapest house in the best street" following the age-old real estate maxim, and we chinked our glasses in recognition.

We found a solicitor in Berwick High Street. She drew up the contract. Settlement (completion) was due in 30 days, and she promised a straightforward process. 30 days was typical, but often parties agreed to a 90-day settlement, as suited. This time frame seemed familiar, coming from the UK.

The solicitor had happy news. "If—you fill in this form, you'll get the 'First-time buyers' grant."

This was worth about $17,000, a one-shot opportunity. As we still had to pay stamp duty—assessed on the dollar—about the same amount, in the end the grant covered it, and it netted off nicely.

Unlike our fellow Brits who had moved to Spain, Portugal or France, we did not have to sit for an interminable reading between the vendor and the buyer in an office. Nor did we need a rubber stamp at the *Marie* or local mayor's town hall. We found it eerily almost too easy.

So, we ended up with an acre of land of our very own, with "room for a pony", and a house. We thought we had won the lottery. At work, my little reveries in the kitchen refilling my teacup extended to the ride-on mower I would get, and the veggies we would grow all year. A "sit-down" one, an Englishman at work said, referring to the business of mowing.

The mortgage agent visited us and sat in one of our op shop chairs and tapped away on a desktop calculator balanced on his knee. He liked the size of our deposit, so the loan required we needed stood at $150,000—which he considered small change. Looking at our meagre possessions, he might have thought he dealt with a pair of penny-pinchers. But we wouldn't get the key until the end of winter.

CHAPTER 18 PLUMBING THE DEPTHS OF WINTER

We crept into our first winter, putting up with the cool days and chilly nights. We got off lightly, really: it sunk to six degrees overnight. We might wake to a frost with the temperature just over freezing with a low-lying mist over the parkland, the sky clear with the stars overhead. Rain came at night, and we'd often wake to sudden squalls and high wind that hit the bedroom window as the low-pressure systems took hold.

You'd think winters would be short, but even Melbourne's drag on longer than you'd like.

I got caught up with work. Kiki got shifts in a Pilates studio in Malvern and taught the older ladies of the Inner East, many of whom asked for her by name. I felt racked by guilt that Kiki had missed out on the warmth of summer I had enjoyed and felt as cold now as she had been in Europe. What stung, though: maybe her London flat had been *warmer*.

"I have never been so cold," she lamented one night.

We had a vintage gas fire lit all evening until we gave up and slunk to bed. Europeans had a common gripe about the cold. UK houses were blessed with double glazing and insulation. In the main, *even in Melbourne*, homes were designed to ventilate heat fast in the summer.

New houses were being built to superior building codes and energy ratings; but chiefly, older houses were draughty. Australians got by with rugs and warm jumpers. Homes didn't have double glazing. Some homes used air conditioning set to heat, known as a "split-system", or used underfloor gas ducted heating.

I looked to my feet, as you do. At nights, they were shod in a natty pair of fleece-lined suede boots that came to mid-calf. They might have been *daggy*. (A word reserved for people with poor taste, such as me.) These were Ugg boots, popular in Australia; people wore them to the supermarket. (Even more daggy.) I had bought mine at Rip Curl, so they were top-notch. They travelled well and people wore them in LA and London. In any case, we considered ourselves up to date with fashion on the home front.

I had found in my first winter in Sydney that I didn't need a winter coat and got by with a fleece. The only time I "rugged up" was at outdoor events when the wind swirled around.

I missed the Sydney winter sun.

***

I found a spider on the architrave one Saturday morning. By all accounts they came in seeking shelter. A big one, too. Its body and skinny legs spanned the architrave, but the smooth body didn't worry me, but I admit when it moved it gave me the creeps. I called Kiki over, and we inspected it, heads tilted to one side.

"Not exactly a tarantula!" I said.

Their hairiness seemed off putting, so this Huntsman did not scare me. They weren't dangerous, but they can bite.

"It's like being punctured with a stapler, an English bloke told me at work," I said.

"Presumably wanting to get one over on you," Kiki retorted.

A huntsman's body may not be ambitious, but the leg span managed a good ten centimetres. One lurked on the ceiling for hours without moving.

"It's come in out of the cold," Kiki said. "I'll relocate it."

Like this one, she trapped them with a cup and relocated them out front, until they found their way back in, and the circle of catch and dispatch continued.

"They keep the fly population down, though," she added.

Snuggled in front of our gas fire, we turned our attention to the television. We got three mainstream channels, seven, nine and ten. These were run by the networks on commercial lines.

The adverts shocked us. We found it impossible to enjoy the climax of a movie when a scene cut to a commercial every few minutes. The canny networks without warning deleted scenes from movies to fit in adverts. Imagine finding Jack Nicholson's speech cut from the pivotal courtroom scene in *A Few Good Men*. We risked a perfectly good movie being ruined at the denouement every night.

Still, we had other options such as the ABC and SBS. The Australian Broadcasting Corporation ran on the same model as far as I could tell as the BBC British Broadcasting Corporation in the UK—no adverts; well-funded programmes, a serious bent. Special Broadcasting Service was independent. Pundits called it "Sex before Soccer" because of the international movies it broadcasted in French, or Spanish. Locals found it almost salacious the things they might watch compared to the "meat and two veg" traditional fare provided by the mainstream. On the radio: "She Will Be Loved" by Maroon Five was a hit song.

We weren't the only ones snuggling. One night, I saw a rat race along the corridor as I walked into the kitchen: the movement caught my eye. I was amazed it had somehow got in but couldn't work out where it had got to. After the shock, we thought it had slunk back outside. We couldn't hear any noise in the roof.

A few days later, I found it in the wardrobe, dead, in my rugby shorts.

"Kiki! Look at this," I called, holding it up by the tail.

"My goodness," she said, grimacing.

"I'm clearly toxic!" I said, and tipped it into the bin outside.

CHAPTER 19 FURTHER AFIELD

We got to the Melbourne Film Festival and saw a smutty movie, in the guise, or rather name of, art. It was called *29 Palms*; which had won a P'alm D'or. A bit much, maybe. As part of the programme, we saw a 1970s cult movie called *Petersen* set on the Melbourne University campus about a tradie who split from his wife and had an affair with an academic. A scene depicted their naked frolic on a beach on the Mornington Peninsula. This leant credibility to my promise it would get warm in Melbourne—eventually. It seemed strange how well-spoken Melbournians were back then, too, with visages of a rather more English accent.

But the test of character was to get out of town and explore more of Melbourne. The city is at the north-east of Port Phillip Bay, with Geelong out west, a city in its own right. The surf coast lay further west still, home to surfers' Bell's Beach where Patrick Swayze and Keanu Reeves had surfed in *Point Break*. (Never mind they filmed in Hawaii.) But we hadn't seen the Peninsula. I traced a finger down the map in a book I had found called *Melbourne and Surrounds*.

The Peninsula ran one way then kinked another. Starting at the city, the *Spirit of Tasmania* ferry waited alongside Port Melbourne pier to embark to "Tassie", a favourite for tourists wishing to see the less-travelled spots of Australia. It was a sizeable ocean-going vessel. Saint Kilda with its famous beach was next, and around the corner, you'd find the Bayside suburbs of Brighton and Hampton. You'd hear people trill "Briiiighton". The speaker told you just how posh they thought it was, affecting an old English accent.

The coast continued to a rather natty marine park and Surf Life Saving Rescue club at Beaumaris. In Patterson Lakes, a series of inlets encroached inland with a launching place for yachts.

Residents lived in waterfront luxury housing in these channels and presumably watched boats come and go as the mood took them.

Then the coast arrived at Frankston.

Frankston got a bad rap. It didn't have the cachet of many of the seaside burbs to the north. Tellingly, people told us it was the location of a Centrelink office where people could claim welfare benefits. The railway line terminated here. I drove down in midsummer and found a bowls club where scenes had been shot for the 2002 movie comedy *Crackerjack*. The green had an excellent view of the bay.

South of Frankston, we would be in Peninsula territory proper: too far away to commute to the city every day, although people brave the traffic if they are game.

Further south, the weekenders got flashier. The road meandered along the coast but there were back highways that could whisk you down faster. Locals enthused about the end of the Peninsula and talked it up as holiday territory. We were looking at dreamy places like Sorrento, and Portsea perched on the final tip. Campsites dotted the foreshore between the water and the highway, and families set up for summer. If they got organised, Mums and Dads commuted to work taking advantage of the shower blocks.

Portsea piqued my interest as it was where the Australian Prime Minister Harold Holt went missing in 1967. No one has ever worked out what happened, and you can keep your stories about the Chinese and a submarine which picked him up; no one knows. As Bill Bryson said in his seminal book, *Down Under* (or *In A Sunburnt Country*), that day Australia *lost* its Prime Minister. *How did that happen?*

We picked upmarket Sorrento as our choice for a day out, and we made a beeline for it. As we stood in the town above the beach, with aquamarine waters as far as we could see, we rather felt we could be Italians. (Maybe I could have been better dressed.) After all, we had our version of the Amalfi coast on our doorstep, and given Italians had migrated to Melbourne this seemed not so fanciful. I could see why the spot was so popular with generations of Melbournians.

The spot faced the quaint town of Queenscliffe across the bay, where the shoreline wheels around to form a circle. A ferry crossed where the two points almost touched. Pleasure seekers jumped on to cross for a day out, when they got Sorrentoed out.

We disembarked the ferry at Queenscliffe on a day with puffs of cloud dotted in the sky. All was quiet on the esplanade and main street, and the Vue Grande majestic hotel stood on a corner. I lost myself in a little second-hand book shop and we gorged on fish and chips as cloud cover increased. Back home, I realised I had still caught the sun and my forehead shone pink.

But the real draw card had to be the revered Phillip Island which was to feature a fair bit in our summers and our lives.

CHAPTER 20 PHILLIP ISLAND

The Island stood in the back bay of Western port, the eastern side of the peninsula. We knew Port Phillip Bay on the city side, but we could find real business on the other side, too.

At 40 square miles, I'd heard no one say a bad thing about it. Smith's beach, a famous surf beach drew surfers and teenagers, and we knew of deserted spots out to the west. It was also home to a racetrack which hosted the World Superbikes Championship every year. Classic car clubs held their concourses there, and drivers took their garage queens out and showboated at sedate speeds around the course.

The southern coast of the island faced Bass Strait, and should you sail, or motor, south several hundred miles, you'd just clip the north-western coast of Tasmania and not shoot through to Antarctica (which seemed a pity.) French island lay to the north largely forgotten. A friend of Kiki's with a private pilot's licence told us she enjoyed flying herself there as a young woman. She said it a thrill to land and take off with no one around.

But the most famous attraction on Phillip Island was a colony of Little Penguins. These were not the King-sized variant of Antarctica, but a smaller, cuter type. They were nowhere to be seen in the day but came back at night to nest, arriving as it got dark. They were so reliable, the tourists flocking daily to the island were guaranteed to see them.

Friends rang us one morning and asked us if we were up to anything. "Come and see the penguins," they suggested. They were busting to get down there to show us. It took an hour and a half there, but they promised us it was worth it.

They said, "We'll pick you up". That sealed the deal.

The highway along the back bay passed the rural farms and little village of Koo Wee Rup and the fishing village of Grantville and turnoff to Corinella pier. Signs announced we were now in Bass Shire.

We had time for a halt at a lookout area on the highway. We scaled a towering wooden gantry to look out at the surrounding countryside (flat, and rather underwhelming). An enterprising man had set up a stall and was flogging fruit. My mate pranked the stallholder by pretending to be a foreign tourist and picked up the wares and shouted unintelligibly in a mock language.

The highway snuck closer to the sea, and I felt as giddy as a schoolboy on a day trip. We approached the bridge over the bay at the town of San Remo, an esplanade of tackle shops, eateries, surf shops, and a pub. We rode the bridge over sparkling calm water, with fishing skiffs and yachts at anchor.

Our friends wanted to show us the seaside town at Cowes which faces the mainland. Passing along near the water, we saw a main strip running to the foreshore and a fishing pier. I could consider the strip as "tourist street anywhere" incorporated, and it had coffee shops, beachwear boutiques, and best of all, an ice cream shop sold any flavour you fancied, as well as lollies. The esplanade continued with fish and chip shops with sea views, and a grass area to sit out on for music events in summer.

We found the "Penguin Parade" at the island's western tip, facing south to Bass Strait. At the timber and brushed aluminium-clad Visitor's Centre, I could see my ticket money was not just funding penguins, but a plethora of tourist stuff tacked on. We funnelled through a turnstile to boardwalks leading out to the sea. The closer, the husher and more reverent the tones of people as they waited, the larger the signage asking us to take extra care of where we stepped.

We found the beach deserted with the sun low in the sky. A series of bleachers had been erected in a semi-circle amphitheatre, and rangers eyed visitors as they took their seats facing the sea. Closer to the front, low down, or high at the back, who knew? Signs reminded us not to shout or use flash photography.

At twilight, we craned from our ring-side seats to the beach wondering when we would see a penguin as the little critters returned from their big day out to their nests in the dunes.

"What do you reckon? Can you see anything?" I asked Kiki.

"Not yet."

People standing up to get a better view were asked to sit by rangers. When it was still light enough to distinguish the line between water and the sands, I saw movement.

Maybe solitary penguins, maybe Mum and Dad, or a village elder? The advance guard? Sure enough, the dots grew more numerous, and we realised we could see entire columns of tiny little penguins—all waddling as fast they could from the sea. As they peeled away up the beach towards us, visitors stood to see.

A sudden cry from a small girl caught our attention.

"Mum, look!" she said.

She pointed to where the penguins disappeared. Alongside the boardwalks, the little flocks walked alongside tourists.

Their little nests were right amongst us.

The little mites were disappearing into nooks and crevices—and under the boardwalk, too. You had to be there to see how excited tourists were. They took photos or stood in a daze. To their credit, the penguins took it all in their stride. It looked like they were used to the attention, a trait that had been passed down through their DNA over scores of lifetimes.

CHAPTER 21 THE HOME OF FOOTBALL

"**A**nd it's all happening at the MCG!" was the common phrase you'll hear when Australians refer to the home of their beloved sport, the Melbourne Cricket Ground.

You'd turn on the radio and hear Bob Lawry, a sports announcer covering sport on a Saturday afternoon. His phrase had entered folklore, as had his exploits as a cricketer with the national team. The MCG was an 80,000-seater stadium for both football and cricket. It had been Melbourne's premier sporting arena for decades.

Kiki and I had wrapped up warm and were on our way to a game of "Aussie Rules" at the MCG with friends, not sure what to expect. I didn't remember seeing it in the UK, but I remember Australian teenagers talking about it when I'd met them. I'd heard it had minimal rules and was rather a "free for all". It has similarities with Irish Gaelic football, but we hadn't seen that either. Were we going to see the big hits, and the blood seen in rugby?

We had tickets for the Essendon Bombers versus the Hawthorn Hawks, two Melbourne teams. 16 teams played in the Australian Football League (AFL). It started as a ball game in the 1850s to keep cricketers fit in the winter off-season. It appealed to women as much as men. It had to be a cliché you'd find a grandmother in the stands screaming their team on.

We could sense the excitement as we walked from the station in a sea of people. The walls of the stadium rose above us to the evening sky, lights illuminating the pitch. We chose the right direction to circle to our gate. Like in a department store, our friends led the way up flights of steps to the level we needed. At our seats, we saw the MCG pitch was indeed monumental.

"It's huge!" Kiki said, shivering in the evening air which

swirled around.

Seagulls buzzed the roof, landing on the grass. All around, fans sat with beer and food, wrapped up warm against the circling draughts. Even Manchester United couldn't attract these crowds, and only the Bundesliga, the German Football league came close.

"I like the shorts!" said Jane, as the teams spilt out onto the pitch.

The players wore shorts and singlets, a "guernsey", and many were muscular, yet athletic. Here were players who could run, tackle, kick and swerve. Both girls looked on in admiration. All of a sudden, rugby and soccer seemed rather pedestrian.

Games played over four quarters, 25 minutes each. Sirens sounded start of play and soon it was on.

"Watch the way these guys jump to contest the ball," I said to Kiki.

It seemed amazing players could jump so high to catch a ball arching through the air. Catching it earnt a free kick. They earnt a chance to hoof the ball upfield to an attacking teammate who only had to catch it himself. If he found himself close enough to the posts, he could have a go at goal.

The most amazing catches were called *"speccies"*, a spectacular. Some of the hits must have hurt.

"GOAL!"

A player scored a goal and ran back, a fist raised in the air. Our eyes were drawn to a TV screen in the corner which had lit up for the occasion. Our ears were assaulted with loud rock music, the bass booming from speakers. It was in that moment we realised Australian sport had borrowed from American football.

The scoring surprised. If a player kicked a goal between two inner posts, he got awarded six points. A miss, but between two outer posts, was worth one point, a "behind". Never mind they rewarded a miss, the shots were from a long way away, and if these boys missed, did I think I could do any better?

The coaches in their boxes could be glimpsed on the huge TVs screens, and I could see their worry. Six poor kicks might net you a meagre six points, over a hard-fought ten minutes, but the opposing team could win back six with a single kick.

If scores are close, no one can be sure who is going to win a game. A single kick in the last seconds can win a game or consign you to a draw or loss. It must have been maddening for a rabid supporter. No wonder Australians could be so scornful of the round-ball "Beautiful Game", where "nothing ever happened". Courses for horses, I guess.

CHAPTER 22 IT HAD TO BE THE ONE

A week before we got the keys, we decided we had better act like we knew what we were doing and inspected the house with "getting to know you" the intent. I filled in an Excel spreadsheet and printed it out at work, so that we looked organised.

I checked off questions. The swimming pool's pump ran at 700 watts an hour which I costed at about 15 cents an hour—it wouldn't break the bank but would cost a bit to run at full bore in summer during the open season. We'd get an efficient pump which ran low and slow as we only needed to turn the water over once a day.

Next, I squinted warily at the septic tank. Now here was trouble, frankly. In most houses, a pipe from the loos takes away "black" (or brown) waste, and no one is ever the wiser. Here, it dispersed into a pit where it decomposed before leeching into lines down the back yard. I saw the way the grass grew well there, grasped the concept of a septic system, and felt a man of the world in the same moment.

The fuse box just inside the corner near the front door looked tired. That had to go, replaced by new circuit breakers. We organised for the transfer of phone, internet, water and electricity. I found the mains water in the front garden along with a tap to attach a hose pipe. It couldn't have been any easier.

I'd love to tell you connecting essentials took weeks or months and that we were under the painful tyranny of the telco and utility companies. I'd prefer to regale you with a ditty of how a customer service rep on the end of the phone made life a misery for us, but we weren't expats starting out in the Bourgogne in France, or on a Greek island. It all went smoothly.

CHAPTER 23 ACROSS THE THRESHOLD

D-Day. We had planned a one-pronged assault on our new place. We received the keys to the house the first week of September. A friend moved our token belongings in his work van up the hill—a secondhand sofa, two armchairs, the TV, a mattress plus our books and belongings.

At the mansion on the corner, the mulberry trees were in full bud; likewise, the ornamental pears were developing shoots. We coasted to the bottom of the valley, our eyes swivelling at the sights. The trees' branches had created almost a canopy above the road which we hadn't noticed before. We parked outside the house in blinding spring sunshine. I felt beyond excited.

I opened the French door in the kitchen and stepped out on the back deck. A flash of colour to my front caught my attention, and a flight of Crimson Rosellas flitted across the backyard from one tree to another. My handy guide *Birds of Australia* told me these were a parrot, a reminder of the climate we lived in.

Yes, the deck needed some love and attention, a sand maybe, but would be fine for now. I stepped onto the grass and walked past the swimming pool to the back yard. It ended in a wooden fence and a gate. Tall gum trees grew on the boundaries, providing privacy from the neighbours. Looking at maps online, we knew the block to our left was two acres, and the one to the right sprawled to three.

I knew a bit about fence maintenance from Queensland: here I spotted the fences on both sides were in good order, thin gauge wire strung between stake pickets. A tension device kept the wire taut.

The tree line at the edge of the paddock marked the half-way point of the block. I found a discernable path, possibly created by kangaroos or wombats. I meandered 300 metres through the trees towards the bottom.

I tripped over a four-cylinder engine from a car. It had rusted, and grass had grown through the piston holes. I couldn't see any sign of the rest of the car, a saving grace, probably. I inspected a dilapidated fence and fallen trees at the bottom. Rot had set in already, and others had grown through each other, their upper limbs entangled. There was no sign of a creek. As I took it all in, I became aware of the feeling we had so much space.

Kiki joined me. "What's that sound?" she asked when we heard a siren.

We looked around until it dawned on us—it was the whistle of Puffing Billy from the Dandenongs carrying over the valleys and re-entrants.

Nights were still cool, so we threw our mattress next to the wood heater. In the excitement I didn't carry Kiki across the threshold, but we *had* found our "forever home."

We walked around savouring the occasion. The traditional tiles on the roof were fine, but the sheen had weathered. In the main bedroom, the walk-in wardrobes were musty, and we left the doors open to ventilate. We looked at the *en suite* bathroom. We smirked at the avocado green and yellow which we didn't take to, but could be replaced. We were glad, though, to have an *en suite* after living European-style *sans*.

We liked the floorboards. The pine continued throughout the entire house—a more up-to-date look—it wouldn't need replacing for years. In the living area we admired the open fireplace, which we thought we'd never use—given we had the wood burner in the kitchen.

The main bathroom was as we'd remembered it. Blue, with 1980s cabinets and horrible, round acrylic taps with a coloured insert in the top. Kiki hanging a mirror on the wall improved things instantly. I nodded my appreciation. We sniggered at the double bed left behind in the spare bedroom. When had it last been made? We had no use for it, but we'd leave it there for guests, for the time being.

Our eyes rested back again on the kitchen, and we became reacquainted with the *mise en scene*. We had been right about the timeless quality. Kiki set the knife block on the worktop.

We had done it.

"Let's light the fire," Kiki said, back in the kitchen.

The nights were still cold. We loved the idea of a real fire, (who doesn't?) and a wood burner known as a Coonara allowed us to burn hardwood at a slower rate than we'd get through in an open fire. I swung the handle and opened the glass door to the firebox and looked at a bed of ash left behind.

To be honest, it was hard going. The wood we had to hand might have been damp. The kindling burnt in no time, and the fire didn't take hold. Smoke filled the kitchen making Kiki wheeze and made my eyes smart. A rush to the supermarket to get firelighters and one of these bundled under dry kindling, and a better choice of wood did the trick.

"Caveman TV!" I said to Kiki, watching the colours of the flames dance.

We noted a built-in fan designed to propel the heat around the house. Turned to warp speed, the sound rattled like the diesel cars of my childhood. The open fireplaces in the living room would have been great, but they can smoke, and a lot of the heat is wasted.

***

At opening time, I presented myself at the hardwood store to order wood to see us through the rest of spring. I figured one load, one-tonne, would do it.

The store had a side entrance to a yard with bays full of mulch, grain, hay, and silage. A man about my age operated a forklift, elbow resting on a roll cage, a flashing orange light on top. I walked past pet food into a general serving area past newspapers stacked on wooden pallets, and a magazine rack. I bypassed the shelves of tools for the buyer who didn't want to nip down the hill and swapped cash for time.

The young man behind the counter in a high-viz top and a

pair of King Gee cotton shorts greeted me.

"Ha ya goin' mate?"

"I'm good," I replied.

"That's the way. How can I help?"

"I'm after firewood please."

"We have redgum, and it's one-hundred and fifty bucks a half-tonne."

This popular species grew in the Riverina area of New South Wales, near the Victorian border. The harder the wood, the slower burning it is, and we didn't want to get through it too fast. People burned "local gum"; wood they found by the roadside, or on their land, or found other hardwood species like Yellow Box.

I confided in him we had been going through a fair amount of wood.

"You need to close off the vent and turn the fan on," he elaborated. "Otherwise, the heat disappears up the chimney," he explained. "But you'll be right."

I thanked him for the tip and grabbed an orange-handled wood splitter I saw in the corner. Surely it would come in handy.

On cue, a truck arrived with a tonne of redgum, and the driver backed into the driveway with his reverse klaxon sounding. I saw him back, keeping a sensible distance. Once he got level with the woodshed, he operated the hydraulic tilt and the tray lurched into the sky. Satisfied he had the angle, he leant over and found a button. The back gate swung open, and the wood tumbled out with a surprising roar. All I had to do was sign for receipt and stack it.

"Do it nicely!" called Kiki through the window as I laid it out criss-cross fashion. "I've got the fire going."

I split a few larger pieces with my new splitter bringing the metal head down as hard as I could. It proved most satisfying cleaving wood in two, hearing the crack and smelling the hewn gum, and I took a few pieces inside. The top plate of the wood burner felt hot to the touch.

"Look, let's close it. I'll put the fan on the lowest setting," I suggested.

"It will warm the entire living area," Kiki noted.

We talked about whether it might be cheaper to buy electric heaters and worked out there was not much in it. Enjoying a fire outweighed the cost. We proceeded on a "pay as you go" basis rather than get an unexpected bill.

It didn't take long to work out a tonne of wood lasted as little as four weeks if we kept the fire going at night, and perhaps six if we let it go out before bedtime. We appreciated waking to find the fire alight in the morning. It had burnt low, but hot, in the small hours of the morning, leaving the kitchen gloriously toasty to walk in to.

We were always looking out for wood to burn. If a tree came down in high wind overnight, locals would be pleased to take off the limbs and cut the trunk into rounds. It took at least six months to dry out, preferably over an entire spring and summer. It didn't matter how wet the wood was, but how *green* it was. Too high a moisture content, and it wouldn't burn. We had friends who burnt unseasoned wood and cracked the glass of their wood burner.

Any tree cut down by the council and left at the roadside could be considered fair game, and men in utes would stop and load it heading back from work. "First-in-best-dressed" was the rule.

You had to be circumspect about tree removal, though. Native vegetation enjoyed the protection of law. You could remove the occasional branch or limb if you were subtle. The council took photos from the air and officials followed up. We could be fined if we took a tree down. If a *"greenie"* lived by, you risked being *"dobbed in"*, told on, and reported to the local shire. We had greenies living just down the street, but they were lovely people.

Winter rain and soft soil would often cause a large gum tree to fall in the night, and locals could wake to find one down in their back yard. It was a good time to arrange a "working bee" and neighbours turned up with the longest chainsaws they owned.

We had to look at it another way, too. Fallen trees were hiding places and habitats for animals, and in theory you needed a permit to move ones that had been lying for years.

CHAPTER 24 REAL MEXICANS

The football season had been in full swing and was in its closing stages when we made the offer on the house. After we had settled in, Port Adelaide played Brisbane Lions in a Grand Final which "Port" edged. They played on the last Saturday in September, a reminder spring was well on the turn. I announced this to Kiki, feeling like a character from *The Lion, the Witch and the Wardrobe*. Only Aslan was not coming.

The giddiness of a new house was eclipsed by a fresh excitement. We planned to get married in Mexico in October. We sat down in the kitchen to go over it.

"Steve, I want to head out the first week of October," Kiki outlined.

"I can't get that much time off work."

"That's ok, I'll go on ahead. You stick around."

So, I dropped Kiki off at the airport, to make plans for the wedding—maybe makeup took a long time to apply in Latin America—I didn't know. She left me alone in our new house, so I had it all to myself for a week. I travelled to work and cooked light meals in the ever-lengthening evenings on my return. When it was my turn to depart, I locked up and left the house keys with the neighbours.

***

The first thing I noticed about Mexico was the smell. The odour reached my nostrils as we prepared to land at Mexico City. Our Airbus floated in a holding pattern stacked in the skies above the ancient city of the Aztecs—what might they have thought of that plague? I soon got distracted from the smell as the pilot extended the flaps, and we hit a bumpy ride.

"Cleared for landing," the captain broke in, the merest hint of tension in this voice. I got tense finding a parking bay at the local supermarket, so I felt sympathy. I mentally crossed myself and said a "Hail Mary"—wasn't Mexico after all Catholic? We had the chance to even the odds up a little. But the smell was not unpleasant nor stomach-churning: I realised I smelt the sulphur and pollution in that metropolis, trapped in the natural bowl of the city.

Of course, Mexico City had been the site of an ancient one long before Cortez arrived with the Spanish. They built on dried-up lake beds, and pumped the water out of surrounding areas. It shared the Venice misfortune of slowly sinking. It is in a natural bowl of hills and mountains at 2,000 metres above sea-level, including volcanoes. I would need to be acclimatised before doing anything arduous. But that was small change: Kiki remembered the 1985 earthquake vividly.

I threaded my way through a crowd—people were shorter than in Europe, the US or Australia. The exit road from Departures swung into a narrow street, and all at once the traffic and sound felt overwhelming. Most of the buildings we passed were concrete. The entire effect: a sea of grey, endless grey; streets and alleyways, but with splashes of colour. We joined a larger road, a flyover with loud advertising on billboards. Like the LA freeways, these roads met other roads on either side, and the roads narrowed and widened without warning. It was a higgledy-piggledy rabbit warren.

We headed for the city centre: a departure after so many years of leaving cities to get home. We slowed at a Pemex service station, where attendants fuelled cars for waiting drivers, all in all, far more civilised than self-service. The taxi turned into a street off the main road.

My mother-in-law waited for us at a front door in the street, the kind of metal door I'd imagine you'd see protecting a prison. She hugged me, glad to see me again. She led us inside.

I found myself in a tiled courtyard with entrances to rooms off it, and an open doorway to what looked like an inner courtyard. In corners, staircases led to a second floor, and a balcony with cast-iron railing above ran around the quadrant. A door led to a living area, including a formal lounge and a kitchen. A maid greeted us and showed us a table laden with soft drink, fruit and tortillas; beef and chicken with salsa. She showed us imperiously to our accommodation through the passageway and up a wrought-iron spiral staircase in the inner courtyard. I was careful not to miss a step and fall flat on my face.

Here, this corner of the second storey looked out on to the city. One way, a door to our accommodation, and another, to another side of the quadrant. It turned out there were eight bedrooms, some in little self-contained apartments. I saw a washing line near the wall ready for use. The maid vanished and reappeared with washing as we unpacked and busied herself with it.

I looked out towards the city and noticed the roof and noise of the service station beside us, a funny reassuring sound of industry. I also took in the view of one of the famous volcanoes that ringed the city.

"I saw a volcano in the distance, Kiki," I said, when I returned to our room.

"Oh, that's Iztaccihuatl—the 'Sleeping Woman'," Kiki replied.

It looked very much like a sleeping woman. I was impressed.

In the morning, I jogged around the block and turned back when the altitude defeated me. I also looked the wrong way and almost ran in front of a car.

I had no idea what was going on most of the time but enjoyed the relative anonymity. I could often be found with a book in a corner. Kiki's family had arrived from California, and her brothers and sisters were staying. One was a well-known actor, with an enigmatic demeanour. I could see he was a man that caused women to fall silent and adjust their hair when he entered a room. Another brother trained as a doctor at Harvard. (This seemed a family tradition, as Kiki's great-grandfather had been somewhat of a medical authority, performing the autopsy on Trotsky long after the Russian met his gruesome death after exile to Mexico City.) A sister worked as cabin crew for Mexicana.

The final sister I knew already: we had stayed with her in Silicon Valley, and she arrived with her husband and daughters.

Clearly any business was conducted in Spanish, and I found myself an unnecessary accessory to pretty much every discussion or activity. After one animated discussion, Kiki turned to me and said:

"Oh, Steve, we've fixed the date of the wedding."

In Mexico, there is none of that business of sending out invites weeks ahead of time. The family is informed and arrives from the four corners—rather refreshing, I thought. Speaking of the four corners: I had called my best man from London, and he was due in the next day.

"I'll be there next week," he had said. He turned up at the airport on time and joined the line of London friends who'd made it over. He arrived in a taxi, and we sank down on a tiled step in the courtyard to catch up. We were in mid-conversation when my father-in-law returned from a local shop and offered us both a beer. The Corona factory lay nearby, and you could smell the fug of hops when driving past.

***

Kiki and I sat in front of the local parish priest with her parents behind us. He officiated at the ancient, white-washed church around the corner near a sprawling market. The market was hundreds of metres square, and you could get lost there if your attention lapsed. To top it all, the local subway had an exit that came up in it. I noted you could also get lost in the subterranean passages under the station where lines interchanged.

The conversation went on for a while, and he and Kiki nodded. Progress was being made. They explained it to me: he requested that Kiki attend confession. And as for my side, I had a letter from my Church of England parish priest in a back pocket which I presented to him. This paperwork was taken as currency and appeared to pass muster, and he re-focused his attention back to Kiki. The reformation in England in the sixteenth century had not been in vain.

The service flew by. I wore my Army "Number One" Blues, or dress uniform; I felt it a way I could introduce a touch of British culture. I had written my vows on a stick-it note secreted in my trouser pocket ready for action. Kiki arrived in a black Audi, and the priest met her at the porch as the organ pounded out the Wedding March (Mendelssohn appeared to be universal). He and she exchanged a few words. My bride processed up the aisle and stopped next to me, and I took her hand in the crook of my elbow. Before the bars of the march ended, our master of ceremonies turned off his microphone and spoke to Kiki once more.

My vows went well, and I heard a slight murmur of appreciation from the congregation when I finished labouring over them. I took Holy Communion: (I did not have the heart to tell the cleric I was not confirmed.) Afterwards, in the sunlight, I asked Kiki what our celebrant had said. Kiki smiled enigmatically and replied:

"He asked me where I had gone to confession, and I replied 'Father Romerio', and he seemed happy enough."

"Right," I said.

"But when I got to the altar and met you, he pointed out: 'Father Romerio has not been there since 1994'."

We discovered the reception had been booked at a country club, and we posed for photos in the gardens and danced to a band. Here, I learnt an uncle had given us his weekend villa for our honeymoon, a lavish place with a swimming pool. I only found out what was happening when a taxi arrived to take us, and we had to pack madly.

Our friends came with us (it was the least we could do) and Kiki and I set up in the master bedroom and landing overlooking the pool, and friends found other bedrooms and sofas around the house. We had no need to fuss about breakfast, as a maid turned up from somewhere and a meal lay on the table when we filtered down in ones and twos. It was here, in the aftermath of the wedding, that Kiki's chief bridesmaid from England met her future husband, Kiki's cousin, and they swam and schmoozed in the pool whilst a gardener edged the lawn beds. We were pleased for them.

CHAPTER 25 SPRING BEGINNINGS

We were a Mister and Missus finally, and so another chapter began. Carrying on the theme of a new start, the plants in the garden shot up, and the beds filled with flowers. Spring sets in quickly in Australia, and a first wave of blooms were seen in August—that's a February day in the Northern Hemisphere. The sun edged higher in the sky at noon and the days got longer.

Kiki loved to sit in a chair in the living room and look out to see the garden in bloom and watch the birds that came to drink in the birdbath. Wattle trees, the Australian flower, were going gangbusters as well as the Petunias.

It was around that time we worked out the "Four seasons in one day" commentary for ourselves. It wasn't just the 1992 Crowded House hit I'd heard at university. A day might start clement and turn to showers. October might be wetter than September, and even on Cup Day—the first Tuesday in November—it might be blowing some.

The Melbourne Cup, a public holiday, was a major race during Spring Racing Carnival at Flemington racecourse north of the city, and the race stopped the nation. The outlandish jackets and dresses also stopped people in their tracks. It was a day out, a chance to let hair down, but we were warned it might rain. A colleague at work said,

"Steve, make sure you take the Monday off, and get a 'long weekend'." It had to be sagacious advice.

Someone told me Cup Day was also the time many people planted their *veggies* or vegetables for summer. They said that tomatoes planted now would take off by February, in summer.

Our neighbour came to meet me at the fence. Chris turned out to be English and had come over from the north in the 1960s. His accent sounded so thick I struggled to understand him, even from one Englishman to another. When I questioned him about the septic tank, he clarified the inspection pit that was foxing me. He had spotted the workmen installing it in the early 1980s, so understood where things were. Our houses were built in 1984 after a bushfire had torn through the village twenty years ago.

On a hot day in February 1983, fires broke out in the west at Mount Macedon, in the high ground in the Ranges there, near Hanging Rock, named after the book and movie *Picnic at Hanging Rock.* The day became known as Ash Wednesday.

"Who fights these fires?" I asked.

"Volunteers!" he exclaimed.

Past the middle suburbs of Melbourne, the Metropolitan Fire Brigade was replaced by volunteers from the Country Fire Authority (CFA).

A director at work told me he had a rental house in our village.

"You have to realise the entire state was on fire, Steve," he explained, flicking his cigarette ash.

On the same day, a fire had broken out near Belgrave to our north and had swept through our village *at 10 pm at night* after a wind change. A fire that had been tracking south-east unexpectedly veered north towards the village. It devastated it.

Twenty people lost their lives that day, as the bushfire tore through paddocks and houses, razing them to the ground, often leaving the chimney stack in one piece as a symbol of what had once stood. Our local fire brigade, staffed by volunteers, had been out all-day protecting life and property, working in the obscene conditions of heat and wind. The fire tore across the main road and a fire truck sheltered as the fire burned through the trees. The crew, including a young Mum from England, survived to tell the tale. One doctor from a house on the top of our hill timed the fire as taking 15 seconds to roar from the bottom to the top.

Amongst the people who lost their lives were the *firies* (firefighters) of a neighbouring brigade who had been sent in to help. They had driven a track in the bush near the hill and were overwhelmed by the front as it passed. This included a casual firefighter who had been helping mates.

It must have been a sore point for the grieving families to lose their volunteers when the men from the village survived to tell their own story. The local community had never forgotten, and Melbournians remember the dust storm that settled on the city and the relentless heat.

***

I thumbed our copy of *Dangerous Creatures of Australia you don't want to meet*, a conveniently sized paper back. I lied: Entitled *Dangerous Creatures of Australia,* it was a pocket edition, useful to carry, to match with dangerous critters you might meet on your way to work.

I knew we were going to see a spider in our new place sooner or later.

"Steve, look at that spider, it just ran past the back of the desk," Kiki said, peering at it.

"Let's see," I replied.

This wasn't a Huntsman, though. It was smaller, midnight-blue, with a tiny white dot on its thorax. I found a match.

It was a "White Tail Spider". I had read enough to know a bite —whilst not fatal, thank goodness—could cause necrosis at the site of the bite. The flesh-eating necrosis could move down your arm, and at least one woman had almost lost the skin off her arm.

More recent articles said the White Tail was miscredited. We had to be circumspect, though, and I dispatched the little thing to its maker.

I drove to the hardware store and bought a can of Mortein which promised to rid us of all pestilence. I sprayed the crevices in the house, the ventilation spaces and door jambs with the noxious spray. I used the whole can. Kiki is not scared of spiders, though. She would rather leave them alone.

We bumped into more neighbours. Many lived on larger blocks of land and had come from farms or had grown up on similar properties and had come here to be closer to the city or work. Many were no stranger to getting their hands dirty, and operated tractors, prime movers and bobcats with ease, and carried out major works inside and out independently. Attitudes seemed different.

There was a lot less of the British "romantic" ideal of the country, where city movers wanted all the benefits of a second, pretty house and garden. They gloried in a flash pair of gum boots, and a real fire at a local pub, but didn't want the hard work. Here, people were "hands-on" in the main.

CHAPTER 26 A PROPER HAIR CUT

"**I**'m going to cut the grass properly now," I declared on a Sunday morning, in the kitchen.

"Good," Kiki said.

Before we knew it, the grass and shrubbery had been going ballistic as the spring sun reached its zenith in the sky at local noon every day. The sun rose in the east, just like it did in Europe, but climbed instead through the northern sky. By two o'clock it was often warm.

Sunday mornings dawned quiet whilst the village dozed after a busy week. Past ten-thirty on a Sunday, Chris across the fence started the first chainsaw or mower, and like a call to prayer, others started up.

Time to cut. God knows what's in that grass.

Not wishing to take a brand-new mower to the long grass down the back, risking dinging the new blades with rocks, or getting discarded lengths of twine in the spindle, I drove to the local servo and hired one I knew I could thrash a bit in the weeds. I loaded it in the ute and secured it with tie-down ratchets.

At home, I manhandled it through the garage to the back. As I pushed and tugged it across the sloping back yard, and piled the clippings in a corner, the appearance of land—our land—took shape. When I took a break, Kiki looked over the decking fence and spotted the transformation unfolding in the bush.

"Wow, it looks like we have *land*," she said, with an impressed note in her voice.

"Doesn't it!" I said happily.

I grinned at her like a loon. It was one of the best days of my life. I had owned my flat in London leasehold, and felt shortchanged, here, we *physically* owned land. I could do whatever I liked, even if it was only an acre.

From then on, we called the section beyond the back yard the "paddock". As Londoners we got the joke, even if no one else did. There *was* room for a pony, after all.

The mower had done the job exposing our block's features; divots and slopes. I saw the occasion I bought my first mower as a red-letter day.

Bunnings Warehouse, Australia's largest DIY chain had to have the answer. Also known as the "Green Shed", we'd find one in every town in Australia of any decent size. Ours was typical as they came. 50 aisles of tools, plants, garden furniture, nails, fixtures and fittings, plus a choice of seat covers for the loo should you find yourself short of one.

The mower aisle had promise. I poured over what I knew were "small engines". I knew the hard choice was between two-stroke and four-stroke. My father would have been proud. I impressed myself, and only myself, by selecting four-stroke. As every schoolboy knew, I wouldn't have to mix fuel with oil, and there'd be less noise. My two-stroke whipper-snipper screamed like a banshee when employed down the back.

I found a *sausage sizzle* (bar-b-que) running a brisk business at the entrance to the shop. These were common at the entrances to all Bunnings stores. The way it worked was that local people representing charities, kindergartens, or sports clubs signed up for a Saturday to raise money. Shifting sausages in a slice of white bread and selling cans of soft drink could net the stallholders several thousand dollars for their cause. (The organisers knew this and limited you to one go a year.) I enjoyed mine with a liberal dose of mustard.

The mower worked out. It cut beautifully and hummed away with a deep tone. I diligently cut a nice line across the top of the jagged edge the *servo* mower had left, and emptied the clippings into a growing, but orderly pile. Chris had seen the new acquisition and met me for a chat over the fence. He wore a Manchester United top and an out of shape hat. He looked amused to see me going so slow.

"Steve, don't bother catching those clippings, mate," he said. "Let them sit where they are."

"See what you mean," I conceded.

I never made that beginner's mistake again and only collected the clippings for the base of the lemon tree when it needed mulching. I also set the cutting deck too high, leaving the grass too long—didn't I need to protect the roots from the scorching heat?

"I wouldn't bother mate," he said.

If I cut at leisure on a Sunday, by Wednesday, it was looking not so gleaming, like a man who gets a haircut for a wedding a week or more before the big day. No local looked for the beautiful lawn: we aimed to knock it back. Past about 10:30 am on a Sunday, if the neighbours in our road and I got out our mowers when we heard the first one, I liked to think we had contributed to a nicer community.

Really, our land was just too big for me to push a mower, but Kiki reckoned it would keep me fit. I planned to mow the back yard weekly, and the paddock every other week, until a neighbour sold me his ride-on mower. I took delivery and rode it up the road like a *cockie* (farm owner).

And as for the clippings. The lemon tree not only benefited, but it also doubled up as a convenient place to go when I didn't want to clump back inside the house with my boots. I did my bit for Kiki's lemons.

CHAPTER 27 THE GREEN SHED

If I had been busy outside, Kiki busied herself with the inside. She occupied herself painting the living area.

The previous owners had been smokers, and she wanted to banish those memories as soon as possible. We couldn't smell any nasty odours, but the nicotine had stained the walls. She got to work; she sanded, and took to the surface with a roller, wearing a baseball cap. She painted a wall around the French windows one colour, and the rest another: she assured me it was still in vogue. This was a "feature wall", and I wasn't bothered if they were still a thing or not. I was happy for her to lead the way.

I went to Bunnings a lot. I gloried in trawling the aisles and feeling useful. I explored and acquainted myself with where things were. The tool shop had to be my favourite. I studied shelving of expensive looking hardware and stood in corners working out what things did. I could buy battery-powered drivers; drop saws with a pivot to make mitre cuts—and an entire wall of drill bits in various alloys. To be honest, it looked mouth-watering.

I saw a display of polished chrome socket sets, some with *one-hundred* parts. I was captivated by an option which had extension arms for undoing tight nuts. It looked the business; and even had a metal carrying handle. In my shopping bag it went.

When you have a hammer, everything looks like a nail. I discovered my ute's oil sump had a 13mm nut, and I now had a socket which matched. I loosened the nut and sent oil streaming all over my driveway, missing the bucket I had placed under.

These were heady days as I got all the things I needed. I bought a petrol blower for chasing leaves, outside (and inside) brooms, wheelbarrows, a hefty mallet, and a bottle of weedkiller called Round Up. I bought two five-litre metal cans, one for petrol, the other for mixing fuel and oil for two-stroke. As my boss said at work,

"You'll be able to know which one is which by tasting them, right!"

"Right," I agreed, but I conscientiously made up a label with Kiki's Dynamo machine.

***

"Steve. I reckon that pool water's going green."

Kiki was looking out the kitchen window. Yes, the sunlight reflected off the pool, but it wasn't quite the blue shimmer we'd prefer. I stood next to her and tilted my head, as if that would make it easier to judge.

"I think you may be right there."

It wasn't far gone, but I knew an algae bloom could take off, and our water would turn a lurid green.

Damn.

I had Googled water chemistry and was all over it. The overwhelming feelings had passed, and sticking with it, I gained a working knowledge. We needed the pH to be right, so that our eyes didn't sting—and so that the chlorine would do its job. And, I worked out the pool shops tried to sell you a whole *"raft"* of stuff you didn't need.

Back at the "Green Shed" I found an entire section devoted to swimming pools. I could choose scoops and brushes that attached to a pole, and chemicals. As of 2022, this wasn't exactly *Breaking Bad*: I needed to nudge the water towards acid or alkaline. The tubs of liquid chlorine looked lethal and made me feel ill, but still: needs must. I grabbed a test kit, which reminded me of the experiments my teachers demonstrated at school.

Back home I resisted the temptation to tip it all in and added small quantities at a time. Actually, that's a lie—I did tip the lot in. The pool turned a brilliant blue overnight. At breakfast, as I stood outside, Kiki looked through the window, gave me the thumbs up and mouthed, "It looks fab!"

The leaves falling from the trees turned out to be a never-ending war, though.

Kiki had also moved outside. She donned gloves, wielded aerators and pruners and looked at the plants. Even more scary—the irrigation systems on offer; connectors, distributors, and taps. She set up a worm farm and added our kitchen scraps for compost. She trimmed the pittosporum hedges out the front door and squashed it in the green bin, jumping up and down in it whilst I held it. When I tried on my own, the bin spun and threw me on the terracing. I thought I had broken my leg.

I needed space to work, so made a workbench for the garage one weekend. I bought framing pine and carried it back on the rack of my ute and beamed as I drove down the Princes Highway. My hastily tied "Truckie's Hitch" held. I assembled it with screws, as I didn't think nails would suffice—and besides, I *knew* I'd bend a nail as I drove it in.

I felt proud though, of the vice I mounted atop. I used coach bolts to secure it and sited it on the left side of the bench knowing being right-handed I'd now be able to work with wood out to my right. For the top, I used hardwood of the sort that goes across doors as lintels. The bloke behind the counter at Bunnings called it "F17". I don't think I ever used the vice apart from sharpening tools, but what did it matter when it *looked the part?*

A circular saw, which took fine-tooth blades for cutting was my next purchase. I tried hammers in my hand for balance and settled on a 20-ounce model. I had seen tradies use tool belts and bought one. If it made them look competent, it made me look like a juvenile, but over-sized Bob the Builder.

"You trying to look like a tradie?" Kiki asked. "What's this, cosplay?"

***

Kiki wanted a dog for company whilst I was at work. My only stipulation: I wanted a proper dog.

We whizzed off to the RSPCA in Burwood but didn't see one

which took our fancy. Instead, we matched ourselves with a cat called Daisy, the poster-girl of the week. We had rescued her from death row, so we felt justified in giving her a home.

Australians have different attitudes to cats. They are efficient hunters and decimate the wildlife. Nowhere is the native wildlife so protected as in Australia and cats, like rabbits, or deer, are considered an introduced species and not natural predators. Many cats never see the light of day outside, and are confined indoors, or roam in elaborate runs owners make, like gladiators on a theme show. We kept Daisy in at night and attached a bell to her collar to foil her chances.

She was a great little cat. There was drama when she went missing—and I made an ad for the local window of the milk bar. She turned up three days later. Maybe hunting was not her thing.

I remembered those early days I was a newly married man and took my marital duties seriously. A colleague stood at my desk with a cup of tea and had advice for me:

"Remember to take the bins out, that's all you've got to do."

"Bin night" was a Tuesday for a collection Wednesday. It didn't matter if you forgot: your memory was jogged by a line of others standing to attention in the road, like a silent convention, when you drove home.

In London, as a boy, I remember the binmen dismounting from their truck and swarming the front gardens picking up bins. By 2004 in Australia, a sole driver operated an extended arm to grab the bin, turn it upside down and place it back. Sometimes I found it sprawling on the road with my shameful chocolate bar wrappers strewn for all to see.

I still forgot, though. I was never perfect in my bid to become Australia's best-married man, and a sharp jab in my ribs reminded me of my failing at 6 am in the morning when Kiki heard the truck.

"Steve, the *bins*!" she said.

It was no disaster, as the truck took ten minutes to go down the side street and return—and if I stood with the bin, in my underwear, the truck stopped. They were good like that. (I'd thank the driver profusely.)

CHAPTER 28 JOINING THE FIRIES

We were getting to grips with life in our village. I found lots to do after a week in the city at work. Raking the winter leaves composting on the ground took a while, clearing the overgrowth down the back and tidying the fence line took longer. Kiki kept up with weeding. Out the front, a little garden had been established in a corner with a little metal archway which led to a landscaped area of delights—all needing attention.

On a still Sunday, I jogged up the road to the township and ran past the hardware store to the primary school, lapped the track —there was no one around—and returned in welcome shade towards the fire station.

Something made me detour on to the hard standing where a bunch of firefighters were standing after training. There were two fire trucks standing on the apron, ready to go, by the looks of it. I introduced myself to the captain who had a red helmet under his arm, and his lieutenants.

"You guys recruiting?" I asked, getting my breath back.

"We're always recruiting," he replied. "Come with me."

Inside the bay, there was a long rack running along the wall supporting two beams. Yellow helmets hang from the top beam, with jackets on the middle hooks. Boots were lined up on the floor, with trousers coiled around them. I followed him into the watch room in the truck bay, and licking the tip of his finger, he peeled off forms from stacked piles, one a police check, all ready for enquiries. I filled them in right there.

"Thanks, Steve, come back in the week–we train Wednesdays and Sundays," he said. "Good to have you here."

I walked the corner to the steakhouse and broke into a jog along our road, picking up the pace, feeling it down the hill. Kiki was in the kitchen.

"I've just joined the fire brigade," I said breathlessly.

She smiled.

Most of the state fire services run volunteer firefighters or "firies". It is the only way to have enough people on hand to fight fires. Most of the firefighters seen on the TV news fighting fire fronts are men and women taking time off from small businesses. Fire season had been declared, and our shire had announced fire restrictions. You couldn't burn a leaf pile in the open without a permit.

To my surprise, though, we weren't on call for bushfire, or to be exact, wildfire. We were *the* fire service, the third emergency service. Residents dialling 000 were calling on *us*. Our remit extended to cars going off the road on a Saturday night: Motor Vehicle Accidents or MVAs; house fires, oil spills; fire alarms going off in the local aged care home, children locked in cars. I didn't ask whether the station had been called on to rescue cats stuck up trees.

We carried a pager 24/7 which would call us to the fire station —the message providing the priority. "Code One" indicated a bushfire, Motor Vehicle Accident, or house fire threatening life (or limb).

Bushfires *really* are a fact of life in Australia. It took me a while to realise that in summer fires burnt everywhere on the continent, fanned by a keen wind. Thousands of hectares, can be burnt in days, and no one will ever see the smoke.

A major cause of fire is lightning strike. Arsonists, too, who took a perverse pleasure in lighting a fire and retreating to admire their efforts. A scant few are themselves firefighters who want to turn up with the fire truck to extinguish the flames and revel in the acclaim.

I read with increasing surprise of two wildfire-prone areas in the world. One was California with its Mediterranean climate, another right here in Victoria in southern Australia.

Right where we were. That surprised me with our cooler

winters.

It was simply the bottom of the continent had dry and hot summers, with low humidity. High-pressure systems trapped over Melbourne below the Dividing range were fed by hot Northerlies—winds coming in off the interior. When Sydney might be cooling off during an afternoon summer storm, Melbourne sat on daily highs of 43 degrees for three days before a welcome cool change came through from the Tasman Sea.

The east coast gets Pacific weather and moisture which reduces the risk. In fact, in Brisbane, in subtropical latitudes, the fire season starts in the Australian spring and ends by mid-summer. The afternoon storms put out the fires.

In 1994, my Aunt rang us from Sydney to tell us fires were approaching the northern suburbs. The air filled with acrid smoke. It was common for residents of cities to see the sky turn orange or smell smoke for days. Fires are unlikely to enter the city as the roads and built-up areas create firebreaks, but running grass fires can attack houses bordering farmland. Big ones roll on through. In 1939, huge blazes on a bad weekend came to be known as "Black Saturday". The fires didn't know to stay away on the weekend of course.

***

On the Wednesday, I got back from work, ate a hurried sandwich, and headed out to meet the brigade. A bunch of men and women turned up from 7:30 pm onwards taking advantage of the lighter evenings. We had academics, electricians, arborists, project managers and teachers from all walks of life. I met an older couple who had built our house in the early 1980s and they were sincere when they regaled me with the lengths they had gone to.

"If you ever want a second storey, we engineered it so you could," the former lady of our house told me.

"That en suite used to be orange. I wanted to see a bright colour after the months of black after the fire," she added with pride.

The burnt terrain must have been glum until the green shoots emerged—like the phoenix from the ashes.

Fighting fire involves putting the "wet" stuff on the "hot" stuff. That came as no surprise. We started by attacking a mock bushfire at a local creek. We pumped water out of the creek and drenched the tops of the trees as if knocking back a blaze in the crown.

To get a feel for the action side of things, I grasped the nozzle, or delivery branch. I shouted: "Water On!" and a colleague leant in to brace us against the pressure. The water lurched out of the nozzle into the trees, pushing me back. I watched the rainbow effect in the water as the evening sunlight flooded in.

"When you're done, shout 'RIGH-TOOOO!!!'"

Righto, I repeated to myself. We used that command a lot. It had a certain *ridgy-didge*—authentic—ring to it.

But the first time I felt I had accomplished anything was when I arrived for Sunday training. Our captain had opened up and prowled the apron whilst an early arrival hosed down the tanker. He saw me park and walked over with a slight limp. This small impediment didn't matter one jot when he could direct operations from his light truck.

"Steve, your ute. Need a favour. There's a fridge going around the corner, and I need it for the station." He jumped in beside me.

We drove out to back blocks and found a surplus to requirements Westinghouse fridge in a shed belonging to a mate of the captain. The white appliance shoved in on its back on my ute's tray, and not twenty minutes later, it provided company for another fridge by the watch room. The captain looked pleased and called for the crew's attention.

"OK, so light beer in the fridge, and now soft drink in this one," he announced.

Cans of pop priced at 50 cents was a perk, and they went down a treat after a morning session.

A neighbour was in the brigade, and he admired my ever-growing collection of tools in my garage when he popped over for a cup of tea. "It looks like Steve has backed his ute into the back of Bunnings and bought half the shop," he told the crew.

CHAPTER 29 DANGEROUS BEASTS

People joked about it. They talked about it. They bought books and swapped stories that approached the reverence of folklore. But really, there was a lot of hyperbole about the wildlife "Down Under". You might wonder if they ever got offended.

Many visitors talked about the dangerous wildlife in Australia. If the sharks and the snakes didn't get you, then the drop bears might. My nieces in California used that as a reason for not visiting for years—I overegged it, maybe. Stingrays had a venomous spiked tail, and the wombat could send your car careening off the road should you hit its armoured back as it hunches on the road. The European wasp could sting like crazy as we knew from encountering them in London as kids. My brother once walked into a nest and got stung multiple times. But we didn't have to worry about the lethal crocodiles we'd seen in *Crocodile Dundee*.

"I've just seen a snake," Kiki said, in a low voice one Saturday afternoon. Her heart was probably pumping.

"Are you sure?" I asked, whispering.

"Look, I'll show you."

I crept out with her to stone terracing in our front yard under the bedroom windows where we maintained bushes and plants.

She was right. Movement in a bush drew our eye, and a reptile-shaped animal darted into cover as soon as it heard us approach. On closer inspection, we realised. She had seen the face of a blue-tongue lizard and not an evil snake after all. I had heard stories of far larger ones scaring the wits out of people.

This one nested in a hole in the brick wall and often came out to bask in the sunshine when all was quiet. It got used to us and I'd often see it at the front.

We also saw larger parrots, the King Parrot, with a green head and a substantial red body, almost two-tone in appearance. One alighted on the pergola beam above or even dared to walk along on the outdoor table, much to the consternation of the cat. She loved the pink galahs, cockerel-sized birds with head crests that flocked in the horse paddocks, and white cockatoos.

Many evenings watching TV, we'd hear the patter of something on the roof above. These weren't European squirrels, or rats, these were possums, a large cat-sized furry animal with impish faces. They were renowned for their heavy footsteps throughout the night. People said,

"You'll know it's a possum, they sound like elephants."

They lived in trees on the fence line, and froze when a torchlight swept across them, eyes gleaming in the dark. At dusk, we'd often spot one hopping along the electricity wire from the power pole to the roof. They caused damage though, weeing and pooing in the roof space when they found a way in. They enjoyed protection of the law and couldn't be harmed, but you could trap them and release them outside. The footsteps, and curious hissing sound they made at night was their main calling card. We once found a baby possum outside on the doorstep, un-self-conscious and sleepy.

Kangaroos in the backyard might be a legend, but not where we lived.

"She's got a few loose kangaroos in the back paddock," was an expression used by older Australians meaning you're not all there. Well, we had a few loose in our paddock. They knew we weren't going to chase them away, and they came to the backyard fence and nibbled on the grass.

One morning, I took the rubbish out and found a baby echidna curled up. (The possum was nowhere to be seen.) It looked like it was waiting for its mother, the poor thing, and I carefully stepped past.

Kiki suggested we walk to the end of the road. So close, yet so unvisited at the best of times.

"Let's go for a walk," she enthused, as I tugged on a sweatshirt.

The road led to a corner where a no-through road sunk down a slope, houses on acre blocks clinging to the hill side, wisp of smoke curling from chimneys. In winter we heard temperatures often fell below freezing in that frost hollow. I saw the paddock on the right awash in spring flowers and pointed them out to Kiki. The tarmacadam road ended in dirt, and our footsteps crunched on it. We scrambled up grass banks when a 4x4 approached us, the driver raising a finger in salute. The land opposite—empty, apart from the home to the family who owned it. It would make a fine pension pot one day when the parcel sold.

After 500 metres, the road vanished into bushland at a set of metal gates with a lock. Only the fire brigade and council workers had access to the old fire trail down. Here, you could bump kangaroos and wallabies (as far as I could tell, they were a smaller version of the kangaroo). Recent rainfall had flowed down the path and created a network of fissures. We halted at an engorged creek which ran and bubbled over rocks, dicey to cross after heavy rain.

I'd often get up early and walk to the creek, slipping a light hooded down jacket on. The hood kept the air from my ears and left me feeling cocooned away from the realities of the morning before coffee and toast. One day, I found a small mob of kangaroos on the grass verge of the road enjoying the sunshine.

Two stood up to each other boxing, lunging forward to attack, then adopting a defensive pose. I had no camera—so I stood and wondered at this presentation of wildlife so close to home.

There was of course roadkill on the roads. On warmer days, the smell was not pleasant. It's easy to spare anyone more details, but a council worker used spray paint to mark the animal to show the pouch had been checked for a baby, which could be given a new lease of life in a shelter. A council worker would collect the body.

It was a devastating day when we saw at first hand that cars and kangaroos don't mix. Kiki told me the story.

She had found a kangaroo struggling in the drainage ditch next to our letterbox. It looked like it had been hit by a car, but the driver hadn't thought to stop. Kangaroos hopped in front of cars, especially at night. They even hopped away early, unwittingly saving themselves, only to jump back in again, often a fateful decision. The headlights confused them.

This one looked terribly injured. A member of Victoria Police arrived in a patrol car and parked on the grass next to Chris's fence. The officer rang local wildlife services, who were busy, and decided there was only one thing he could do—and drew his service pistol.

"He was standing there, arms out, trying to work out where to aim!" she said.

A kangaroo whilst as big as a small adult is still a small target, and the policeman wanted to make sure of a chest shot, as he'd probably miss otherwise. A small crowd of neighbours had joined.

"It was awful," she continued.

"What happened then?" I asked.

"The policeman put the kangeroo out of its misery, and the council took it away."

***

One afternoon, I strode through the gate into the back yard. I wanted to head to the garage to get fence cutters. Imagine my surprise when I came face to face with a snake.

Its head was level with mine. It coiled up on the slope above me: you could say it had the high ground advantage. I looked around but Kiki wasn't around.

I knew all snakes in Victoria were venomous. We knew the Red-Bellied Black snake is venomous but not aggressive. The Tiger snake, on the other hand, *is* aggressive. Many Australian snakes are not the gargantuan thick-bodied rattlesnakes you see in movies—or in Africa, or Asia. If anything, they run on the short and skinny side, with small heads and tiny fangs.

Regardless, they are amongst the most dangerous in the world. Not all snakes will envenomate on strike, nor deliver a lethal dose. But if you got bitten, it was no time to make assumptions.

This one was unmistakably a Red-Bellied Black. I stepped back and detoured past the pool playing it safe.

The snake catcher arrived in a white van, armed with a pronged spear and a backup net. He walked the property—then he crawled under the deck, a narrow enclosure if ever I had seen one. He appeared overeager, even a little excited. We had likely seen a Red-Bellied black snake.

He didn't find it.

What he *did* find was the ditch on the side of our road as he reversed out of our driveway. To this day, he is the only person to have ever done that in 20 years. He returned the next day to have another look. He was an enthusiast and wasn't leaving empty-handed, but he never found the snake.

CHAPTER 30 THERE'S A STANDARD OF SORTS

I attended several weekends of training that spring before we hit fire season. "Minimum skills" placed an emphasis on safety. Permanent instructors wearing blue short-sleeves employed by the fire service ran the course. They covered the theory with PowerPoint presentations in classrooms in the fire station, followed by practise out the front on the tankers. If we got wet, that was a sideshow.

The instructor clicked on a presentation on his laptop, and a series of slides appeared.

"Let's talk about safety," he said.

Volunteer firefighters had lost their lives in a "burn-over" situation out west in Linton in 1997, and the authority realised no common training was in place.

The firefighters who died in 1983 in that reserve up the hill from our house were also caught out in the open when fire tore across the track they had ventured down. Lessons had been learnt since. Modern tanker cabs are equipped with fire curtains to protect crews in the several minutes it took for fire to burn over.

"You must leave a quarter of a tank for yourselves. Always," impressed the instructors. My captain didn't mince his words about radiant heat.

"It will kill you," he said, matter-of-factly, shrugging.

They taught us the basic wildfire skills we needed to defend our towns. I listened to the instructors carefully. We had to learn how to pump water from dams or swimming pools and out through the delivery hoses. The tanker carried 2,000 litres, which gave us minutes of "attack". The first firie attacked the blaze and in those precious minutes, others connected the tanker to the nearest hydrant.

A firie in a house might be needing that water to save a life.

***

I never forgot the first "turnout".

I was on the phone to my bank in the UK wrestling with the vagaries of a funds transfer. My pager emitted a sound I couldn't place at first, and I looked around wondering (*was it the smoke alarm*) until I joined the dots and found it in my pocket. The display said:

FIRE1 CODE1 STRUCT HOUSE FIRE Brighton
Road Flames and smoke seen

I breathlessly informed the client rep:

"I'm off to a fire," and hung-up.

She might have wondered what sort of firefighter conducted bank business during work hours.

I drove to the station making hasty and sloppy gear changes. My heart raced, and the adrenaline coursed through my body. The turn on to the main road was without drama, and I made it to the station car park. Another firie had got there just before me and had opened up: a bay door had been swung open, and I ran through.

"Let's get going!" he cried. I ran alongside the clothing rack to find my peg. I struggled in to my "yellows", checking my gloves were in my pocket. I'd be needing them.

I climbed up into the passenger seat in the cab, and two other firies climbed on the back just before we pulled forward.

"Ok on back?" I asked on the intercom. They replied in the affirmative.

The firetruck lurched out on to the road, dripping water. Passing motorists saw the flashing lights and halted to let us out: a local we knew gave us a wave. Chatter from the radio on the VicFire channel came through speakers in the cab. I picked up the mike and put a call into the control centre.

"VicFire, this is Tanker One turning out to structure fire,

Brighton Road." The girl from control replied instantly:

"Roger, Code One."

That was the confirmation we could go "Code One" with lights and sirens, under those road rules. Technically, we could break the speed limit, or go through a red light.

She continued. "Further information, Tanker One, we're not sure how bad this is, but Police have been responded. The call did not come from the property."

It was useful getting this extra information, especially if the dispatcher still had the callers on the line.

We had barely got a kilometre, when we were turned back. It was a "False alarm—Good Intent." I grabbed the mike and realised there were other fire stations on the net.

"VicFire, this is Dandenong Pumper turning out to a Motor Vehicle Accident."

"VicFire, this is Rowville Rescue One on scene."

I had to wait until no other station spoke, and then I took my chance in the middle of the radio traffic.

"VicFire, this is Tanker One returning."

"Thank you, Tanker One," she replied, not missing a beat.

Back at the station, our driver backed the tanker into the bay, and we dismounted. The captain had been in the second tanker to turn out which had got back first. He stood in the bay.

"First turnout, eh, Steve, well done mate."

I was back on the call with my bank half an hour later. It took me awhile to get that adrenaline back under control.

The calls came at the most unsuspecting times, often before dinner, although I don't think I was ever on the loo. I figured the dispatcher who organised the 000 calls wanted to observe some sort of decorum.

I became proud of my ability to respond with "less haste, more speed". I figured the people who dialled 000 appreciated it. I kept my trousers coiled over my boots at the front door, so I could step in neatly; and my jacket and helmet hung at the station. With practice, I got there in three minutes, my eyes on the speedo.

I found it fiddly responding to the turnouts at night. One night, sound asleep, I struggled to get out of the bedroom and bounced all over the walls trying to find the door. Kiki might stir and murmur, "Drive safe." No time for a kiss. It was a serious business after all. Did she ever worry? I understood any concern, yet she kept her fears to herself.

I'd often get back after the "false alarms, good intent" calls, and realise I was still half-asleep. It led to surreal night jobs. We giggled at people's pyjamas: our captain had a few choice sets. Most nights we returned during the night and slunk back into a warm bed, on others the dawn greeted us, and we chatted wearily by the trucks before heading home.

I got to know the members of the brigade, an eclectic mix of people from the area. Some lived nearby and could respond in under a minute, others lived further away, or were social members only and came up for monthly meetings for a cup of tea and a vanilla slice. The captain, a retiree, lived just outside the village who had time to put back into the brigade. We could find him at the station sorting who had which pager, or ensuring all vehicles were ready to go.

The strangest things caught fire; we attended a ride-on mower that was ablaze—I guessed a fuel line had burst. And we had the time a man flung petrol on a "burn off" wood pile and received third-degree burns. He called the ambulance first, and all we had to do was put out the pile. Our man was in the shower under cold water with the ambos in attendance. He was led out into the evening naked with plastic bags to protect his burns, and we turned away to preserve his modesty. The ambulance whisked him to a specialist burns unit.

We were once called to a house by the dispatcher and told to park up at an address and consult police "already in attendance". The police commander passed on we had joined a hostage scene. A man had threatened to set his house on fire with himself in it.

We spent a good hour there before the police released us: the man didn't set himself on fire, and he got the help he needed. It was a good outcome for all.

CHAPTER 31 SUMMER GOES ON

"**I** *do* like this Sauvignon Blanc," I said, taking a sip.

"Yes, it's a good one." Kiki replied, Maui Jim sunglasses on her forehead.

It was a warm December Sunday, and a white sun beat down under an azure cloudless sky. We had no relief from any breeze and the laserlight on the pergola roof creaked as the temperature rose and the joists expanded and gasped.

I reached out and refilled my glass. Next to my feet I had a bottle of white wine. Not just any bottle, a bottle from the Marlborough area of New Zealand touted by *The Australian*'s wine expert James Halliday. His eyebrows were as extensive as his experience.

I had acquired a huge *eskie,* an ice cooler. This one was of gargantuan proportions. The sticker promised me 100 litres. It fitted as many bottles, or cans of beer or Coke as you could imagine. In the bottom I had laid a bed of ice from the servo, which sold it by the bag. (All you had to do was rock up and self-serve. What fun!) The local supermarket sold it too.

"We wouldn't be dead for quids," I said. Another Australian expression I had learnt.

***

Christmas seemed a lot less commercial in Australia. Sure, it had to be the same in many ways, with the local malls packed with people scavenging for presents, and the supermarkets were full of people buying food to feed the five thousand.

"Fancy seafood?" I asked Kiki.

"Love the idea," I replied.

Lots of Australians love the idea of a seafood platter of King Prawns, Moreton Bay bugs at Christmas, or a feast on fish like Barramundi. No one wants to be basting a Turkey on a hot day or slaving over sauces on a laden stove top. I liked crunchy calamari —"squiddy", seasoned with salt and pepper.

We noted though, overall, there wasn't the same mania for Christmas as in Europe. As I said to Kiki, Christmas was the curtain-raiser for the summer holidays and people moved on swiftly to the rest of summer. I did note the summer theme, Santa portrayed on a Christmas card on Bondi Beach, Father Christmas sweltering with his reindeer struggling too.

Our first "Aussie Christmas" was spent with friends. We had friends over on Christmas Eve for a bar-b-q. My pager sounded, interrupting our chat. A bushfire had broken out in the Cranbourne Botanical Gardens, twenty kilometres away. I dropped the tongs and ran.

We took the firefighting ute, with a small fighting ability with 400 litres of water, used for "mopping up" and "blacking out."

A lieutenant and I arrived at the station first, and we drove "Code One" down the hill to the suburbs. We shot through a red light in Berwick, and I glanced at my driver to check he hadn't taken leave of his senses.

When we arrived on scene, we found the fire under control and needed blacking out. A helicopter wasted no time in dropping water to contain a smouldering edge. I was standing on the flank of the fire when the crew returned with another cargo of water. The loadmaster in the helicopter gave me the thumbs up. It was funny, or a shame, depending on how you looked at it, when I got soaked in the water cascading down. He had given me fair warning.

It was good to get back in time to see in Christmas night with our guests.

Our friends hosted us for Christmas Day. It was a warm one, not that this was guaranteed in Melbourne. It was refreshing to share the day with another family. After lunch we waddled with full bellies to the local oval to play "backyard cricket", preferring to field in the shade. Here we were, with the opposite weather we'd expect. Boxing Day was of course a public holiday. Lots of Australians watched the cricket on TV live from the MCG, the traditional five-day "Boxing Day Test" against a touring side maybe England, the West Indies or South Africa. If it was England, then the test match would be a big one, and thousands turned out to it full of Christmas pud.

***

The New Year arrived. If it had been warming before Christmas, now the heat had truly arrived. Summer days in the office at lunchtime were hot, and we risked sunburn if we sat out long. I ensured I had my baseball cap. After several pints at lunch, I often inadvertently burned the back of my neck. Kiki had something to say if I did.

The Australian impressionists noted by summer the unforgiving sun washed out colours. The fields of Ireland were famed for dark green hues, but here, fields took on a washed-out lime green with the heat.

We were on the deck again.

"What do you reckon to my hat?" I asked.

Kiki looked up. I had gone to Ray's Outdoors and bought an Akubra hat to replace the old one after I ran over it with my mower. I had trundled to the neighbour's front yard to tidy it whilst they were away water-skiing, and a gust took my old hat clean off and under the blades. It was the Australian slant on the cowboy hat with a broad felt brim to protect the face from the sun.

"Very nice." She had one which she took with her tool bag of trowels and twine. "I'm off to prune."

By mid-January, I realised:

God, it gets hot in Melbourne.

Getting into the car was amusing. Left in the sun, the interior had been super-heated, and the steering wheel was hot to the touch. Those first few minutes were uncomfortable until the AC had cleared the air. Better still, was finding a tree to park under.

The spring days which struggled to get to 19 degrees were now routinely 32,33,34 degrees, or more. The temperature climbed, then just when you were getting sick of it, it might rain—but we were grateful. The cold front was often explained as a "south-west change", as cooler weather came in-from Antarctica, presumably.

We felt the change come in as a welcome breeze. At work, haggard, and sweltering colleagues opened the weather website and looked at the wind direction and observed temperatures. They tracked the progression of the front as it moved west to east from Geelong towards us. The wind direction flipped from north to south-west one after the other. If the change hit the city by the afternoon, it was approaching us thirty minutes later. On a hot day, it was glorious to sit at home and feel the relief of those light breezes.

***

"Hi Steve. How's it going?" said Chris when we met at the fence line on a Sunday afternoon, furtively. It felt good to be resting in the shade there, sweat trickling down my calves into my socks.

"Hate them," he said.

"Hate what?" I replied.

"The leaves, I spend all my time raking them."

I looked and saw what he meant. In the warm breeze, leaves were cascading off the trees and they caught and snagged along the fence line. They stuck in the drainage ditches out front and under the car windscreen wipers. They named an Australian Christmas Carol "The North Wind is tossing the leaves" and a line referenced brown grass in the paddock.

This is exactly what was happening. Not only were the seasons reversed, where December was now summer, but summer breezes were now playing havoc too. It wasn't just autumn where leaves dropped off the trees. Soon a willow tree down the back—now there was a pest, with roots growing into the septic tank field—would be laid bare.

I picked up the leaf scoop from under the pool decking and picked recalcitrant leaves out of the water. A feature of native trees: it was common for trees to shed ribbons of papery bark too, and they went in the green bin too.

The evenings promised to cool, and if I had the window open, the first of the welcome evening breezes wafted in through the fly screen as the outside temperature dropped.

CHAPTER 32 TOTAL BAN & BARBEQUE

"Ok, do we have a bush fire plan?" asked Kiki. It was yet another hot day.

"Ah, yes, you saw the sign too, right?" I replied.

The sign on the road to the village broadcast we were in the fire season, yes, but firies had put out extra signs that today would be a "Total Fire Ban Day".

On the days when weather was forecast in the high thirties, with high winds, these days were declared. This meant no fires in the open. Gas barbeques were allowed, but you needed a bucket of water if things got out of hand.

We were on high alert for smoke in the neighbourhood. Even the welcome changes might bring problems. Stormy weather arriving in the evening might bring lighting which could spark dry bush and ignite a grass fire.

People activated fire plans on those "bad days." Their bags were packed with non-synthetic clothes and blankets that wouldn't melt should a car be caught out during a burn-over. Tradies avoided working outside on roofs. People closed curtains to keep the sunlight out. There were lots of near misses even if people and property were not affected. The fires could burn in a remote location like the Alpine for weeks. The focus was on building firebreaks downwind of the blaze, and where it was likely to travel before it got to regional towns. The worry of the fire commanders and the State Premier was palpable in those times.

***

BLEEP! BLEEP! BLEEP!

My pager had gone off—again.

INCIDENT1 CODE3 Infant trapped in car

I cancelled the warning. This looked like an interesting one. Code 3 meant no immediate threat to life, but we were dealing with a child.

We got on scene in the tanker, and I let myself down from the cab carefully. A Ford Falcon sedan car was parked up outside the community centre and a worried-looking mother waited for us.

"I've trapped my daughter in the car, the keys are next to her," she said to the lieutenant.

We looked inside and saw an infant about twelve months old strapped into a baby seat. She seemed unstressed, for now. The problem was the rising heat of the morning. So far, the back of the car was cool to a bare hand.

"Have the RACV been called?" asked a lieutenant.

"Yes."

The local RACV would respond from the car garage in the main street so would not be long.

"There's no point in breaking into the car if we can gain access shortly," said the lieutenant. "What's important is your daughter. If it gets warm, we can cool down the car with water." He looked at me.

To illustrate this, I took out a nozzle from the equipment locker.

So far, the infant looked fine.

The RACV driver turned up in a vintage Ford. It was striking that motorists relied on such an old car to get their much newer cars going again. He had the door open in minutes, going in through the door strip. Another successful job done.

***

"So, what shall we do for your birthday," Kiki said. "Why don't we have a barbeque?"

"Right, let's do it," I replied.

"As long as we don't throw a shrimp on the barbie," I continued. This popular saying was a myth, apparently.

It would be seriously amiss of me if I didn't jot down my

thoughts and experiences of outdoor cooking. Barbequing is part of the outdoor culture in Australia. We would provide the meat, our guests brought what they wanted to drink.

I studied the barbeque which had been bequeathed to us by the previous owners. It seemed legit enough. It was in the classic everyday mould: four gas burners side by side under a metal plate and a metal grill. We'd cook onion on the plate and do steaks, sausages and burgers on the grill. A hefty gas cylinder sat below on a shelf and supplied gas via a rubber pipe to a screw connection.

Anyone can place meat on a grill and watch it. The skill is all in the prep; the care and insouciant attention required. Kiki said she'd take care of that, and she marinated the meat overnight.

"So that's done. Over to you, Steve," she said. *No pressure.*

My job was to cook it on the day. A mate from work came to assist. He took one look at the barbeque and told me I needed a boost on the heat side.

"Steve, got a tip for you, you'll need more heat," he pointed out.

"Show me, let's go shopping," I replied.

At Barbeques Galore, now that was a veritable feast of gear— we bought a replacement metal plate to slip over the burners. My mate explained we'd add ceramic chips which would radiate additional heat. I thought it a capital idea. At the servo we swapped out my old gas canister to ensure we had a full one.

"You don't want to run out halfway through!" he warned. "And who knows how old that one is."

It might have been called Swap N' Go, but it was touch and go whether we would be successful.

The teenager on the till with a bit of down on his upper lip looked at my canister. "Not too rusty, mate."

I sighed with relief, and he got the key to the cage and exchanged it happily.

Our friends arrived, and we spent the afternoon in the pool and munched on lamb chops and steaks. I had a baseball cap on, and a beer in my hand. It was a hot one, and the temperature climbed steadily. I sunk chest height into the pool with my t-shirt on and felt the water cool me down. It turned out a roaring success, and my colleague suggested if I scrubbed the barbeque now it would be all ready for next time. I squeezed myself out of a chair and looked interested.

If there is a next time, I thought.

I tell you what: I saw the way more serious players operated. Australians don't take it as seriously as say the South Africans, or the Argentinians.

In fact, Argentinian friends invited us to Noble Park to show us how it was done. They had built a brick barbeque in their back yard and cooked on a metal tray. Above the metal tray a joint roasted, rotisserie-style, skewered on a spike. Uncles stood by, taking it in turns to police the meat. There was a definite spectator element to barbequing.

Kiki was not so keen on barbeques. We were told they attracted rats. I didn't skewer anything on a rotisserie, but used the grill, even in winter, and got a special barbeque jacket to wear. If I had been a reformed smoker, this would have been the time for a cheeky cigarette.

So, whilst flush from the success of our first proper Bar-B-Que, we wanted to play it safe and have a fall back. Which brings me to other attractions.

We knew of a startup vineyard around the corner, and we paid it a visit on a Sunday afternoon, timing it just after lunch when orders were just tapering off. The venue was sited on land just back from where the main road intersected the back route I'd found. The local pub backed on to it, too, so the two properties were tail-to-tail, partners in crime.

Rows of neat vines were arranged in lines over 20 acres of sloping landscape. We noted the delightful setting featuring a bull-nosed outbuilding that had been turned into a front of house for the punters. The *bullnose verandah* had entered the Aussie design vernacular. We saw the characteristic, snubby, metal roof that poked out over the front, forming a verandah. It perched above decking to provide protection from the sun.

Inside, in the gloom, we found a small shop. The wall was racked with bottles, and uncorked bottles on silver trays lay on the countertop. A teenager dressed in black greeted us solemnly and led us into a back room with large oak vats eight feet high. The floor had been sanded back to bare boards with slight gaps, leaving our shoes to pick up a fine dust.

"How good is this?" Kiki said, to use a local expression.

We rolled up our sleeves and tucked into olives and fresh bread drizzled with olive oil. When the pizza arrived, we had long washed the bread down and were hard into a bottle of fragrant Chardonnay.

CHAPTER 33 LIFE AND DEATH

Being a firefighter didn't give me a licence to wear flash gear, nor attend hen nights, more's the pity. The CFA issued one pair of "yellows" which were neither offensive, nor flattering. It was a one-piece cotton coverall. The real prize though, was a large blue "turn out" padded wool jacket with a yellow "CFA" tab across the back. It might have been 2004, but the technology was last seen in the 1970s in the US and featured in the flashback scenes in the 1980s movie *Backdraft*. Australia was well behind the US in this aspect. But the gear had to do.

A large proportion of our 000 calls in the Brigade were for cars that ran off the road on the way down the hill. The road twisted and turned, and a few corners had become notorious in the wet. It was normal for cars to spin off into trees on a Saturday night.

We secured the area, blocked the road, and allowed access for the *ambos* (ambulance)—if so required—or even the SES State Emergency Services to help extract cars from ditches. We had basic tools for this job, but they were the specialists, and we might have been needed elsewhere. If it was raining, the police preferred to sit in their patrol car out of the inclement weather and leave traffic control to us.

Cars had been found on their backs in the tree canopies, occupants unscathed. I once arrived first on scene and had to maintain watch over a woman whilst the ambos checked her. I had a charged hose in case the car caught fire: a spark from metal on tarmac might ignite spilt fuel. I can still remember the look of distress on the poor woman's face. She didn't need me standing there to remind her.

It was the fatalities that challenged us. At 2 am, one night, I attended a scene where a car with young men had hit a tree. The car looked a mess. The solid tree would stand for many more years, witness to the accident. The impact killed the young driver outright, and his passenger and a man were trapped. I got there with one of the girls, who drove—the immediacy of the situation meant we drove "two up"—just the pair of us. Saving life and extinguishing fire had to be the priority.

I found it unsettling to watch the car whilst the State Emergency Service cut into the car to gain access, slicing through the A, B and C pillars of the car. When freed from the back, the young man's response was to scream. This was a reaction to us moving him. Crush victims could die later after the toxins from their wounds were released into their blood stream. The prognosis could be bleak.

We closed the road and diverted traffic to another side street. The scene was illuminated by lights, and it took on a macabre dimension. The traffic we had funnelled down the side streets drove by carefully, and I suspect, craning to see. It would have been spooky to see the blue and red lights strobing through the trees.

Back home, it was light, just before breakfast. I laid on my back on the bed, arms locked behind my head and looking up. When Kiki came in with coffee, she saw me staring into space, with a thousand-yard stare locked in.

"You OK baby?" she asked. "Were they alright?" She turned to straighten the bedclothes.

"Dead," I muttered.

"Really!?" she replied, spinning around and leaning over.

"Yes." I had nothing more to say.

What I didn't tell her was that I couldn't get the poor dead boy's face out of my head.

I felt sad seeing the injuries and loss of life. One girl was on her way to her mother for Mother's Day and had stopped to get McDonalds. She had been wrestling one-handed with her hamburger, but got her foot stuck under the accelerator and lost control of her car near the first corner. She was killed on impact.

A local tradie had driven inebriated and had hit a tree on a back road at about 2 am. The impact had sent a metal coupling through the back of his cab into his head. We found him injured and breathing, when we turned up, but he died soon after from the trauma and blood loss.

"I need your help getting him out," said one of the lieutenants.

We got him out of the cab and awaited the coroner who was several hours away. The body had to be protected, and we carefully turned a corner of a tarpaulin over him. His father arrived with a policeman, and we turned around and stood away, respectively, remaining silent. After he had gone, a member of our brigade was upset when someone plugged a kettle in for a brew.

"What are you doing, do you think this is the time to have a cup of tea with this bloke here on the ground?"

He didn't think it entirely appropriate. He got his reply soon enough:

"We've been out all night. We still have to drink, mate."

***

The basic wildfire qualification was rudimentary, but this didn't qualify you to attack a burning building and especially not enter one. That was another course entirely.

"OK guys, if my house is ever burning, I don't want you three blokes in there," said the instructor, looking serious as we took off our Breathing Apparatus masks, and helmets, the sweat beading in our hair.

We were down at the CFA's training ground not far from the bay. A full-sized facility was available, and the designers had thoughtfully considered the delights to offer trainee firies. The lengths they had gone to was almost Disney-like. There were cars plumbed like a gas bar-b-que designed to light up to simulate a car fire, but another installation was called the "Temple of Doom".

It was a concrete tank that tested our ability to enter burning buildings, find, and drag out residents. The interior could be configured any way the instructors pleased, from one day to the next, so that we wouldn't learn the layout. We had about 40 minutes of air, but with our lungs sucking it in, it was more like 20 minutes. We wore distress units on our shoulder straps that emitted a beep every few seconds. If one of us became immobilised, it would start emitting a distress signal and flash.

On initial runs, we disappeared into the smoke holding on to each other's air cylinders but as we advanced, we learnt to spread out, and to head straight to the places people could be, mindful of the seat of the fire, but still in support of our teammates.

"You guys have failed. I need you back here this afternoon," the instructor continued.

I looked over at the guys who had come out ahead of us. They looked crestfallen.

"There was not enough teamwork, guys, you were all bunched up."

"You guys, though: I want you in my house." He looked at us.

On the last run, I could just about see the head-torch of the firie to my right. I found the 80kg dummy on the floor and we dragged him out along the hose line back to the door.

"I liked that, fella," said the instructor. I nodded and moved to prevent my distress signal sounding.

"How much air have you got left?" he asked.

I looked at my gauge.

"110 PSI," I said.

"Great. So, you could go back in for another search. Remember, any less and you can't go back in."

I nodded again. When that pressure got to 40 PSI, a loud horn went off telling us it was time to retreat from the building. *Time to get out.*

Overall, I enjoyed my time with the third emergency service. We didn't get paid, nor expected to be. Other firies in other states received expenses or payment, but it never occurred to us to ask. The reward had to be the experience and the sense of giving back to the community. Many loved the idea of driving a big red truck. I loved the whole application of it all, the intensity of training and doing something *real*. And never knowing when the call might come, day or night.

PART B

CHAPTER 34 BERT NEWTON SUPERSTAR

Kiki rang when I was at the office. I found myself right in the middle of an exacting conundrum, deep in Excel hell for a report I needed *toute suite*. Did I need square brackets around that pesky formula?

"Darling. Guess what."

Guess what.

"What." (I had a sixth-sense, an inkling, I knew where this was going.)

"I'm pregnant."

The split-second pause seemed like an eternity. The heavens opened; cathedral choirs sang, and rainbows yawned handsomely all in an instant. We were both excited our lives together were to enter another phase.

"That's great," I enthused.

Drinks at lunch were raucous, and the skin on my shoulder was laid sore, if not open by the slaps of congratulations from my colleagues.

***

Getting practice for sleepless nights, I was called out of bed to a house fire the next weekend. This was serious business, and I attended several over the years. My pager told me the news:

FIRE1 CODE1 STRUCTURE1 21 BellBird Road 21

One of my friends joined me in the tanker, and it pulled forward to the road, waiting for the traffic. A lone car halted to let us out.

"How you going, Steve?" he asked sleepily.

"Good mate, Kiki's pregnant," I replied, tightening my helmet strap and finding my gloves and ensuring all my pockets were done up.

He grinned and shook my hand: we were momentarily distracted from firefighting duties in those moments before we turned our attention back to the job.

Before we arrived, we smelt smoke and heard the flames. The house was fully involved, and unsalvageable. The brief of the fire service was not to save a house, but to contain the spread to the properties next door. I grabbed a coiled 64mm line off our truck and manhandled it up a rise to the front door for use. It was heavy, and I stumbled a bit, still sleepy, hoping no one saw. One of the guys clearly had enjoyed a night cap, and he weaved around a bit.

The homeowner had left a saucepan on the hob which set fire to the exhaust above and spread rapidly. I got back in the early hours, checked our stovetop, and sunk gratefully into bed.

So, with Kiki being pregnant, I ensured she was appropriately pampered and looked after. I watched out for the appetite and cravings; I held doors open for her. She wasn't easily defeated.

We attended a few pre-natal appointments. I felt like I had entered a sitcom. Full suburbanisation was in the wings ready to envelop me. I was no longer newly married. It seemed we had moved on, a tick-tock towards domestic bliss. I came home to find her on a chair taping the cracks in the doors with foam to prevent draughts.

A friend and neighbour soon put a stop to that. "Steve, she can't be up a chair like that!"

I explained she was dealing with an ex-elite dancer. "Kiki will push herself to the limit to achieve what she wants to achieve."

There were many times when I let her do things her way.

***

Kiki called me at work again.

"Guess what?"

"What?" I felt glad of the interruption from a gnarly issue I had been wrestling with.

"You know the Bert Newton show?"

It was a show that occupied a precious morning slot on one of the networks. It might have been Ten.

"Yes…" I replied.

"Well, I've got tickets for the audience."

"How much did you pay for those?" I asked.

"I didn't—they make so many seats available per day."

"I guess they fill them, then."

But I was in, "like Flynn".

At the studio, we were ushered through to a waiting room where a funny man dressed in a hat waited. He looked vaguely familiar. I think we both realised simultaneously. We hadn't lived in Melbourne long, but we recognised him as a comedian on the circuit. He had appeared on stage at the Comedy Festival just gone. He kept up a light patter.

I saw his job was to "warm us up" so that sleepy, even nervous, audience members had the required happy faces. The producers don't want stone faces and looks of boredom; they wanted their prime-time daytime viewers to pick out a sea of glossy, engaged faces.

Not only was he funny, but his lines reminded me of the old chestnuts from my childhood in the UK. And as in the military, I had a retort, or a few extra lines for him, and people laughed.

"Hey! *I'm* the funny one," he said, handling me sensitively and professionally.

Kiki looked at me and rolled her eyes, knowing me all too well.

Our seats were not quite in the front row but near a camera, and I felt my brow glisten under the lights. It was a little unsettling, and warm, in our ring-side seats.

Bert Newton's eye scanned his audience and his eye rested on Kiki's bump, her pregnancy clear as day. He approached us flanked by his co-star. A production assistant out of shot advanced too.

"Are we expecting?" he asked on prime morning TV.

CHAPTER 35 WAH WAH AND POOS

Pre-natal care and the health system were going to be a minefield to navigate. In ways, we were lucky neither of us had any experience of the UK to compare it with. We had no pre-conceived notions as first-time parents, just like owning a house on a block was new to us.

The first major decision we had to make was whether we were going to go private or public.

We believed the Medicare public health system in Australia to be excellent, but we paid at the point of service in other areas, for example, dentistry.

We chose public. We had discovered the local hospital in Berwick had a maternity wing led by midwives. This segued well with Kiki's wants. A friend of Kiki's explained if we chose private, not only would we be up for all the premiums, but we were outside the "waiting periods" too. Kiki wanted a natural birth, and the midwife approach resonated with her. A midwife knew a birth was supposed to be tough, and Kiki could get through it with the right encouragement.

We attended pre-natal classes. One class outlined what Kiki and I might expect once labour started, and I paid extra special attention. I enlivened these with little jokes which made everyone laugh, although I admit not as much as me.

***

I picked up my father- and mother-in-law from the airport. They marvelled at the start we had made together. My father-in-law loved the countryside, fresh air and took in big lungfuls, and stared at the big sky. My mother-in-law, never one to do nothing, whisked around and took over the cooking, the remarkable woman she was. Our second spring was upon us, but there was no sign of a baby.

To chivvy things along, Kiki walked the two kilometres from home to the local steakhouse. She would have needed to plod the uphill section and then enjoy the respite under the shade of trees. I was at work, but ready to rush back when I got the call.

With no news, I joined them at the restaurant in time for a main course. Getting carried away, my father-in-law and I shared a bottle of wine and were studying the dessert menu earnestly when Kiki realised she had just had her first contraction.

"Boys, I think we have to go," she said.

"Why?" her father said.

"I think I'm going to have this baby."

I dropped my in-laws off at home and whisked Kiki straight to the hospital. We had been told to expect her first labour would be a long one.

Kiki didn't want to be distracted, so she sent out the staff and refused to have them in the room. That included me, too.

I walked the ward, wearing a hole in the carpet. It's been years since men were not required to be in attendance, but Kiki was going to do it her way, even if it meant the professionals had to stay clear.

A full 24 hours elapsed before we saw our baby. She was born at about 8 pm the following night. I knew we were near as the staff crept up out of sight to the door hoping not to get caught. There had to be *some* oversight. Kiki allowed us back in the room just in time for the birth.

She was a tiny baby just over 6lbs, just shy of two kilogrammes. She had sparse blonde hair on her head. I popped home and brought the grandparents over to the ward, both beaming. We found it rough as the baby made up for sleeping the first day by not sleeping for most of the next week.

CHAPTER 36 PARENTHOOD

My father-in-law doted on the baby. He swapped between making faces at our daughter and idling on his back in the pool. It was still very cold, but he couldn't wait to get in. Kiki did her best: and settled into regular feeds. Our little baby drifted off to sleep most evenings. To encourage her to sleep, Kiki used to bounce her up and down on a Pilates ball. Sometimes it worked, often it didn't. What we weren't prepared for was her waking every night the first year. It was rough.

Just before Kiki's parents went home, we were driving past the general store after lunch, only to find a car ablaze in the car park.

"Better get to the station, Steve!" Kiki said, parking a safe distance away.

I looked both ways, and dashed over the road and we were back with the truck minutes later. Kiki and her mother looked to see what would happen next, and my father-in-law held the baby. I put out the car fire, show-boating a bit, whilst Kiki's mother took photographs.

"Stay clear!" I shouted. "The diff might go bang!" I had been told differentials can explode and whizz out from the car.

At nights, I put out car fires whilst Kiki fed. It was all in a day's, or night's work.

Parenting was good. The opportunity to grow up on acreage within striking distance of a capital city was a prize in Australia when so many kids grew up in the suburbs. Ours was 18 months old when she saw her first snake. Another Red-Bellied black. We stood next to the pool decking and watched it crawl away to the safety of the tree line 40 metres away. She pointed down the hill but didn't quite have the words to describe what she saw.

***

Our second daughter was born, nineteen months after our first.

Kiki took them both to Mexico for about three months. I stayed at home as I couldn't get the time off; besides, an air fare was $2000 return . Later, it became cheaper to fly and we might pay $1000 return to LA. It was an opportunity for them to see their grandparents, and introduce them to their aunties, uncles, and cousins. They picked up Spanish by osmosis and paraded past the market and the street vendors to kindergarten, immersed in the culture.

A boy arrived, a brother for two sisters. He had blond hair too,and bright blue eyes taking after his paternal great-grandfather. I felt smitten with my boy, but took them to creche one day a week. My favourite time was picking them up. They would look up from their activities and come running to my open arms.

"Daddy!!!"

One day, I came home early and got called to a house fire, so I dropped them off at creche to be taken care of (I was on my own). I turned out "direct" to the property on a back road hidden away in the trees. The entire house was alight, and the distraught owners were in tears. There was nothing we could save, but I left as soon as I could. I arrived at the creche wearing my fire brigade t-shirt, surprising the receptionist with my face and neck blackened from soot. It was special to see the kids.

Kids had a great life in Australia. It was a prime reason migrants set up there in the first place. There seems to be a magical, even mythical, dimension to growing up in paradise, where time seemed to have slowed (or never caught up at all).

Our kids loved the pool. They could spend all afternoon in there once we had slathered them with sun factor 30: 50 if we had it. As a child, we talked about sun-tan lotion and Factor Eight seemed cautious. Here, we called it *sunblock*. In summer, the kids wore hats, and polyester swim wear to ward off the UV. There were excursions, too. One day, at Melbourne Zoo, I crouched to point out a lion and stood back up next to Grant Hackett, the Olympic swimmer.

We'd visit the houses of other parents with larger blocks where we found even more to do. Parents supplied small motorbikes and quads, and Dads gave the kids rides on their mowers and trailers. It wasn't unusual for kids to be on their own dirt bikes before they started school.

There were sleepouts in the warmer months with firepits. The kids slept under the stars.

Kinder was a fun time characterised by "Show and Tell": maybe taking turns to share a soft toy. By the time they started "prep" in school at age five, they were well socialised.

"No hat, no play!" Kiki announced, one morning.

I scratched my head. "I can't find it anywhere."

Luckily, we had a few on hand.

The school year started at the end of January after the summer holiday. We saw Christmas as the curtain raiser for the long break. If Christmas at the solstice was a pagan event in the Northern Hemisphere: all two days of it, here it was time to take serious time off. It felt like a fresh start for everyone.

We took the kids camping. Australians love the outdoors, and that's anything you care to name—fishing, jet-skiing, cycling, or canoeing. But the greatest love of all, the great leveller, is the camp. It was popular to Easter school holidays book ending the season's end.

We were still getting to grips with the seasons being upside down. By Easter, Autumn had got its foot in the door, but March and April in Melbourne is often the best time of year. It brings warm days and sunshine, and it often stays dry. The heat of February had subsided and was already a memory by then. Families hitched their trailers and hit the highways to beach towns all along the Victorian coast to the New South border. More ambitious families took their kids out of school for a year and drove the entire coast, looping the continent.

Kiki said, "Have you seen the stuff people buy!?"

We could go nuts, and buy a 4x4 like a Toyota Land Cruiser, and a garage full of gear. There was a raft of extras: solar recharging panels, air compressors, and a host of things on special from BCF, or Ray's Outdoors. My favourite was BCF which stands for "Boating, Fishing, Camping". An advert tagline dreamed up in a lunch hour by an ad man ran *"BC Effing Fun."*

We stuck, though, to the basics of a tent, chairs, tables, a gas stove of the sort fired by a barbeque gas cylinder, cook set and plates.

Our favourite camp lay on the peninsula at Sorrento on a dune overlooking the sea. The kids ran amok and enjoyed toasting marshmallows on a fire.

CHAPTER 37 THE BEACH HOUSE

Many people took another approach and bought a beach house. But as the locals said, like the swimming pool of lore—*the best one is the one belonging to someone else.*

The really swish beach houses sprawled down the Peninsula from Mornington onwards. We were glad, though, to be invited to Phillip Island one year to stay with a family. Many Melbournians own a beach house there. We didn't know it, but this was to become a fixture.

You could say the beach house lay *within cooee* of Cowes where the population swelled during the tourist season. We found it tucked in a quiet block of streets near the shore. All towns on the island are named after those on England's Isle of Wight; Cowes, Rhyll and Ventnor in an unabashed reference to the "Old Country".

The house was raised on stilts, clad in HardiePlank weatherboard. A rickety staircase led to a deck. Inside, a simple living area and galley with three bedrooms, a master, twin, and a bunkroom. We had TV, and a bookcase stocked with paperbacks from op shops, each with a previous owner's name in the frontispiece. Under the house, a little flat with a shower area and a double bed. If you asked me, it looked like a breeding ground for spiders. The good-sized back yard had a creaky metal mower shed with a padlock on the door.

We came to love the beach there. We liked the one nearby, within walking distance with bags and towels. Another was further away up the road and we took the car, or I took our dogs before the day's heat arrived.

We accessed the closest on foot via a short course through trees and dunes. We had to pad along blistering sand, hot to the touch. If you lost your thongs, you had to do a little dance on the spot as you burnt the soles of your feet. A wrong turn could end in a tangle of brush. And if you didn't lose your thongs, then the rear flicked sand into your back.

We never got sick of the sight of the beach; it might be busy, other times we got it to ourselves. I jogged from one end to the other, enjoying the sensation of the sands under my feet. I'd stand thigh-deep in the water and look across to the mainland on the other side of the channel whilst the kids braved the surf, my son emerging like a Greek God whilst my daughters struck impossible ballet poses.

They say in Australia that the beach is one of its factors in its lauded egalitarian life; that in your *togs* or *swimmers*, no one really knows what you do for a living, or "for a crust"; whether you went to Geelong Grammar, Balwyn High, or Dandenong school, whether you are the manager of a hedge fund or work for the council and pick up the bins. The beach is a great common denominator and leveller.

We'd jump in the sea, and then dry out in the heat in minutes under that lethal UV. Getting burnt was no fun. We bought a shade umbrella which we could twist into the sand and weigh with a bucket of wet sand. The sun edged across the sky over the afternoon, and we adjusted our towels accordingly in the shade, the umbrella a makeshift sundial.

"So, here's the order, Steve," Kiki said, handing me a page of notepaper.

"Righto," I replied.

All I had to do was collect it from Rhyll fifteen minutes away.

Fish and chips had to be as popular "Down Under" as in the UK, and we chose a place at Rhyll, ringing in the order. I'd jump in the car to collect, windows open, hand out in the breeze, returning with the boxes steaming on the passenger seat.

I can't remember when I first learnt what basic fish and chips was. Fish is "flake", and it is *shark*: not the angry, shouty Great White, or Mako, but the little Gummy shark; a small one you can catch on a rod out in the bay. It was *good eating* for the budget conscious. Spend a few more dollars more, and there was Blue

Grenadier or Barramundi to enjoy. They asked you if you wanted your fish fried or grilled—prepped with batter, or without. In the London fish and chip shops of my childhood, I recalled no choice —you got fried fish.

Another popular destination could be a slow perambulation down the road to the ice cream shop which sold ice cream and refreshing sorbet. My tastes in ice cream ran to a childish setting: bubblegum, pistachio, and licorice.

I supervised the kids with ice cream like a boss. I made it my specialty to police melting ice creams, and if necessary, intervene with a lick, or a decisive bite which often ended in tears. Either that, or the ice cream ended up on the pavement— guaranteed to end in tears, anyway.

We often saw in the New Year down there in our happy place. On New Year's Eve, we walked along the foreshore in the dark towards Cowes to see the fireworks. If I returned to work, Kiki took the kids for a last hurrah—when the crowds were less manic. We liked it in winter when the beach lay deserted, and you'd have the place to yourself. Before we left to head back up the Bass highway, we wrestled with the lock of the garden shed and mowed the back yard; trimmed the bushes at the entrance and raked.

We came to adore it over the years, and the kids treasured it.

***

Gippsland. The gateway to country Victoria. A land of paddocks, dairy country, wire fences stretching into the horizon, boutique vineyards and artisanal cheese factories, mostly quiet, but with a rush-on at Sunday lunch. Also, people who had sold up in Melbourne for hectares on a river to grow vegetables, and emailed their work into a city office.

One Easter, we arrived at the gate of a small country property on 20 acres. I pulled off the Princes Highway and headed through two small towns, at one point threading through a field under crops, one a lurid yellow.

We found the house down a long winding road from a small town dotted that way (we ran over a snake on the way), and we pulled up at the gate. The house cladding appeared to be singed black in places. A bush fire had come through and a firefighting helicopter had come in, like the calvary, at the last minute and saved it. I liked the sweeping spaces front and back, and at the side—an orchard, nets strung across the canopies to protect the fruit from fossicking birds.

We found the entrance full of old Driz-a-Bone waxed jackets and riding clobber, garden tools and wellies, and a bench to take off your boots when you came in so that you didn't bring dirt inside.

We inspected an interior, untouched or renovated since at least the 1970s or 1980s bursting to the seams with character. We noted two living areas: one had been turned into a study full of antiques, tapestries and art.

Come into my boudoir.

The furnishings and curtains draped and swished. We felt the substantial effort that had been put in to make the place feel loved. I admired a huge ornate desk covered in papers. with fat teak legs, but well-turned ankles. I had a sticky beak and found swimming pool cleaning instructions, incongruous with the dusty dog-eared paperbacks. The kitchen had an entire array of hald-empty whisky and liqueur bottles on the countertop, and in the main bathroom, a sunken area with a bath to step into.

Overall, the house was rather esoteric, and looked like a scene from an Agatha Christie novel or Indiana Jones movie. We were smitten.

Next to the orchard, a dam flanked by trees. I had bought the rods, and we tried fishing, and I made a real pigs-ear out of it; I think I put the kids off for life. The property had views of sloping meadows to a forest where a railway line had passed through, now decommissioned. It was now the site of a rail trail, or bicycle track unseen through the trees.

Friends joined us, so we lit a bonfire out in the orchard, collecting and dragging fallen limbs for a fire.

CHAPTER 38 PITCH PERFECT

As a boy, I had sang in a choir soaring to the heights of head chorister, as well as those high notes. My voice changed when I was 13, and my soprano notes were gone forever. In fact, apart from sessions in the shower, I never sang again in front of an audience. A good thing, maybe.

But that all changed when I joined a Melbourne-based choir. Firefighting was all very well, but I needed another outlet.

Queen's College was at the north end of the city CBD, part of Melbourne University. Not quite the dreaming spires of Oxford, it nonetheless gave its best attempt at an old-world mix of collegiate tradition. The brickwork and façade had been built in the nineteenth century and a grass-covered quad slumbered at the back. It opened in 1889: the time of Queen Victoria's Jubilee and provided halls of residents to science students. The choir met here once a week. A fact I found alluring: it sang with one of Melbourne's premier symphonic orchestras.

I had a sneaking suspicion I was a tenor, and this was confirmed on the first night, when I sat next to a "Bass 2" (or Bass-Baritone) and found I did indeed prefer the higher register.

Our choir master was a charismatic leader with his own entry in the Australian *Who's Who*. We hadn't met, but introductions were complete when the Bass stood and announced to the room "Got room for a Tenor at the front, there?"

I was re-positioned at that front in the Tenor section and never left. The Tenor section was the smallest section in the choir, as well as the rarest voice type. True Tenors are as rare as rocking horse poo, and we enjoyed the status afforded us. We also made more than our fair share of volume, our higher registers dominating. In fact, when I made my way home on transport, I found young students parted, saying "It's one of the tenors." I felt like José Carreras.

And the choir was a good one. Just about everyone could read music, and there was no repetitive note-bashing. My new Bass friend told me "We are probably the second-best choir in Melbourne, only behind the Melbourne Symphony Orchestra chorus." That sealed it for me. *There was a standard.*

"We are *singers*, not buskers!" reminded our maestro. Accuracy was important. Whilst there was no audition, anyone not making a standard would slip away. The pace was frenetic.

In high-billing performances, we sang in a chorus with soloists and up to one-hundred musicians from brass, woodwind and string. We assembled in our evening dress all over town, at the Melbourne Town Hall, Hamer Hall and Federation Square in front of a thousand people. The stage lights bore down with an intensity, and we felt compelled to give our best as we competed with the volume of the orchestra.

Carmina Burana, *Mozart's Mass in C*, Verdi's and Fauré's *Requiem* were mainstays. We launched CDs and shot Verdi's *Requiem* for DVD. There were radio and TV commercials, and Prime Minister's Olympic Galas, even an appearance with John Farnham on stage. To hear the sibilant rustle as a member of the audience unwrapped a Mintie sweet during a quiet moment of string made me laugh.

***

But the highlight was providing backing singing for the Edinburgh Royal Tattoo when it arrived in Melbourne. The old Telstra Stadium we had seen football in had been renamed Ethiad when the airline took over sponsorship. They transformed a section to stand in as the real-life part of Edinburgh with a fibreglass castle erected at one end.

We endured four live events, 40,000 people spilling in through the turnstiles each time. I found it nerve-wracking we had been miked up for Channel Seven for broadcast. The arena was large enough the accompanying sound from the massed bands reached us with a delay. The solution was to rely on a "click-track" synchronised with the TV broadcast which we heard in our earpieces. It was daunting to hear ourselves resonating all around the stadium.

Breaks between shows were a chance to warm up, but sleep, too, in an armchair. We shared ground-floor rooms with a Scottish dancing girl's troupe who flounced around in leggings and activewear. They might have been bothered with our warmups, but equally, it was exhausting to see them stretch.

The experience was beautiful and mesmerising.

CHAPTER 39 CUP DAY VEGGIES

In London, a friend lived in a street backing on to woodland to wander in. I would drop by to see what his latest project was. It invariably involved machinery, tools, disassembled parts, greasy fingers and a whole lot of muck and effort which I didn't want a part of. It was interesting seeing what he had achieved. Perhaps his finest hour was the day he bought a chainsaw. Hardly a conversation went by without him inserting his new toy into it.

But I realised one day I needed one to cut up a fallen tree down the back. It had to be a few weeks' worth of firewood going begging. What to do? I needed a chainsaw. Mates had pointed out two half-decent brands: Stihl and Husqvarna, and I had a budget north of $600. I chose a Stihl with a 16 inches bar which I got from the dealer down the hill, wanting to buy locally.

I set it on the garage floor and looked at it the way a man looks at a captive snake.

It was worth taking seriously. Two men in my fire brigade had missing fingers, both chainsaw accidents, and whilst they were happy enough blokes, I bet they'd prefer to have all their fingers.

As luck would have it, the local men's shed were organising a course and so I attended to listen to a retiree pass on a lifetime's experience of chainsaws. The shed was cavernous, well-equipped, with industrial-grade tooling and machines; from lathes, to thicknessers and drill presses.

The fella instructing looked like he had a lifetime's experience dealing with machinery, and wore a baseball cap over greying locks, and glasses. He had cuffed his socks over his stretched and worn boots. We stood in a semi-circle in front of him. He coughed for our attention.

"Listen in carefully, fellas. It's simple really. The chain." He looked around. "Gotta be a sharp one."

We craned forward to watch his demonstration as he scraped a file along the teeth. I think we understood the key takeaway, and I tried it with him watching. He grunted. "You're not going hard enough. Look, let me show you."

I came to a new understanding as our master cut his finger when testing the sharpness. He insisted my chain was, likewise, lethally sharp, and badgered me until mine reached his high standards. Only I remained unblooded.

"What are *they*?" Kiki said.

"Protection," I mouthed, bending to adjust my trousers. "Fifty bucks on eBay. I'm going to cut up that tree."

I had won an auction and received in the post a pair of chainsaw safety trousers. These had steel fibre in the knees and shins. An errant chain would catch in the material and snag if I slipped. I didn't need an imagination to know the trauma if the teeth took a chunk out of my leg.

"OK. Good luck with it."

"Do me a favour. If I'm not back within fifteen, come and check."

Emboldened, and having received my instructor's blessing, I pulled on the starter rope and the saw murmured. I turned off the choke, and she started on the next pull. The teeth of the chain ripped through the boughs with ease and threw bar-oil and dust on to the ground.

I had reason to be wary: chainsaws could kick back when making undercuts (I avoided them), or pull out of your hands when making overcuts, and cause you to stumble. I discovered I could get the chain stuck in sappy wood, which took untold might to extricate as sweat beaded on my brow. After a session of sterling work, the chain blunted, so I called it a day. The diligent worker would sharpen up the cutters before next use, but I needed a beer.

***

Leaving home to go anywhere, I charged up the hill, foot on the gas, steam coming out of my truck's exhaust on the cool days. I'd enter the avenue, at the top, marvelling at the properties either side. I learnt there was always something to gawp at, like the old codger at number 47 who was always out spraying the weeds in his drainage ditch.

Opposite the turn, we had a small reserve. A dirt track led into a valley. A circuit was about two miles, and if I tacked on the climb from home, it was about three all up. It was the perfect regime to buff up legs and get the heart and lungs going.

I loved the runner's exhilaration, and solitude. My feet thumped against the leaf litter on the track. I was always on the lookout for Fallow deer, or even the revered Sambar in the thick vegetation.

The loop came out near the main road to our village, and I walked alongside, the traffic whizzing past. If this wasn't interesting, the secluded track I darted back into was—the scene of a murder in the 1980s. It must have been before the sole house down there got dogs, as they barked as soon as they heard anyone.

Burying could be a theme. We planted vegetables, hoping to see life emerge from seeds. Two approaches were available: truck in earth and build boxes, a "No Dig" approach; or prepare the ground by digging. Kiki chose the hard way, but she had the foresight to bring in a Ditch Witch under the supervision of a neighbour. She knew the benefits of mechanical advantage. Whilst I was at work, it motored up and down the paddock excavating, and soon we had a veggie patch.

We planted tomatoes, capsicums, zucchini (courgettes), potatoes and lettuce. Brassicas like cabbage and broccoli did well in winter. We remembered to plant tomatoes around Melbourne Cup Day. If our horse did not come through, the seedlings might later.

"Steve, the tomatoes will go nuts in February," Chris said, standing amongst the seedlings I had dug in hopefully.

And, the zucchini had to be seen to be believed. They often

added half-a pound overnight in the summer nights. It seemed like Black Magic.

I once looked down the backyard, which meant Kiki had a project brewing again. The war of attrition? Defence in depth? Was I considering the anniversary of the Battle of the Somme, in the First World War?

No. We saw the flock of hens that had moved into new quarters in the backyard. We converted an old children's cubby house into a stronghold against any fox looking for a quick meal. On any given Sunday, it was possible to see a snout looking over a bush eyeing-up supper.

Neighbours lost chickens all the time from their yards. The cycle of life and death was all part of animal husbandry as far as they were concerned. But a fox could come in and create havoc in minutes and could lay waste for the shear hell of it when only one hen made a meal. We hoped to outsmart it, by layering in barriers, and dug mesh wire into the ground 30 centimetres deep. On some mornings, you could see where a hungry fox had dug and given up. I don't think we ever lost a hen, and most of the time they succumbed to old-age.

The cubby house had to be the Taj Mahal of *chook* houses: painted white, with a trapdoor that granted access down a flight of pine posts into a run. The hens had an automatic feeder to dispense seed when they hopped on, and as much water as they could drink.

We took payment of course; eggs in lieu of cash for the five-star accommodation. The hens laid in external nesting boxes, and we only had to lift a lid to take delivery. Service was reliable for the first few years of a hen's life and then Kiki allowed them to live rent-free.

On this morning, they scratched around in the yard and tugged the grass out to my annoyance, but it didn't keep the grass down.

Kiki sniffed. "There's a bit of a whiff!"

This wasn't the chickens. She said, "The septic tank is getting smelly."

On warmer days, the aroma hit your nostrils fleetingly. We knew the bare mechanics of a septic tank when we moved in. The sludge broke down in biological action and leached out in a field to evaporate in the paddock. We couldn't be sure how efficiently this leeching happened, and we had reason to suspect —not very well. Same shit, different bucket.

CHAPTER 40 FIRE

We were in full child-rearing mode, but that doesn't mean Kiki and I didn't get out of the house. We were always up for a trip to the city. We'd find babysitters and get out to dine. One night we chose the Press Club on the corner of Flinders Street and Exhibition owned by a TV MasterChef judge. We made a solemn pact we wouldn't be overawed and that we'd act like the sophisticated diners we were (or had been). I wore a shirt from the London shirtmaker TM Lewin (I still bought them by mail order), and Kiki looked divine. The dark mood matched with deep, sumptuous leather seats and wooden chandeliers.

The degustation menu was a delight as we worked our way through courses washed down with a bottle of wine, with water to cleanse the palate. A waiter popped up on schedule to talk us through each stage. He was absent, later though, when the young man on reception talked us through the $400 bill.

We enjoyed after-dinner drinks at a whiskey bar on Exhibition Street or even the Butterfly Club behind, which attracted a diverse Burlesque crowd. The venue had several levels with bars serving, each floor with a different décor. On one, the wall was covered with picture frames. In another, there were movie posters, and we watched the crowd. But we had to get back to relieve the babysitter.

***

BLEEP! BLEEP! BLEEP!

My pager made a racket. I sprung upright and grabbed it from under my pillow, peering at the display. How routine was this going to be?

FIRE1 CODE1 STRUCTURE House Fire on Blaxheath Road.

This looked like a big job. I stepped out of bed and found the door handle. Kiki looked sound asleep and did not stir. I opened the front door, and stepped into my yellows and boots, and the diesel engine in the ute clattered into life. I had been awake for mere minutes when I made the turn at the end of the road—no traffic from the right at this ungodly hour—and reached the fire station 30 seconds later.

I unbolted the station bay doors and hauled myself into the left-hand seat of the truck. A lieutenant hauled himself into the driver's seat. I put in our turnout message to control, noting we had made our time limit of four minutes.

"Vic Fire, this is Tanker One, turning out to a structure fire, Blaxheath Road."

"Roger, Tanker One: Code One."

The duty responder replied with more information.

"Tanker One, the building is full of smoke, not fully involved."

This sounded promising.

The driver leant over and turned on the lights; but didn't bother turning on the sirens. The blue and red lights reflected off the eucalypt gums as we flashed past in the dark. It was always eerie, and otherwise silent, apart from the woosh of the engine and the gasp of the brakes as we took the corners. It took another three minutes to arrive on scene. Seven minutes had elapsed since we had been responded.

"Tanker One: on scene, now known as Blaxheath control," I said.

"Roger, Blaxheath control," the dispatcher replied.

We found the owners waiting by their front door, wearing woollen beanies and in the clothes they had found before stumbling outside.

"Glad to see you guys!" they said.

"What's going on here?" said a lieutenant. He clearly had some grasp of the situation but was gaining more information.

"There's smoke everywhere. We think there is a fire in the roof space," the man said.

"OK, we'll take a look," the lieutenant replied.

I strode to the Breathing Apparatus locker on the side of the truck. I pulled hard on the rack, and two hanging sets of apparatus pivoted out of the locker. I backed in and put my arms through the harness and pulled to detach the unit. I checked the pressure. 210 PSI was good. I left the mask hanging around my neck. My oppo grabbed the second set. We walked to the house.

"There's an elevated walkway to the second storey here," the man said, indicating a flight of steps.

"Ready to go in?" said another firie who'd arrived in the second truck.

I nodded and activated the Distress Signal device. The firie had placed a full 38mm hose at the doorway. It was charged, full of water. I'd be needing that. I grabbed it in a gloved hand, and we entered and found ourselves in a smoke-filled room, proceeding cautiously. It was hard to see where to go. In movies, firefighters can see through thick smoke and flames. Ominously the heat started to spike, and as we made our way closer to the fire, we saw plastic dripping from an air conditioning unit above our head.

We had to get out as soon as possible.

Our third truck had arrived, followed by a truck from another brigade. That backup crew with a ladder had gone into the attic. They figured the fire was in an attic bedroom accessible from the eaves. One firefighter smashed a hole through, and the brigade renewed their attack from there. Depending on your point of view, we found it amusing when a brigade member fell through the attic roof, suspended only by his armpits.

At dawn, we rested out the front of the property sweaty and weary. The light showed two Swiss Alpine style properties on a slope from the main gate. The light flooded the hillside and showed us a beautiful property, with a well-tended lawn in a little valley. It was breathtaking, and we allowed the view to wash over our weary bodies.

As for our fallen firefighter, he felt sore for a few weeks.

***

Sore losers weren't welcome at the poker groups I attended locally. A bloke I had met at the local branch of the RSL (Returned Serviceman's League) for veterans had set up a table in his shed, and a group played monthly. The bloke was always in a rumbunctious mood and scrutinised every round. I was a new player and had to learn the rules on the fly. The difference between a Flush and a Straight: whether I needed to count four or five cards in a row—and whether to play a hand or discard it early. (Craning forward to count was not a good look.)

Many of us needed glasses to see the suits on the cards. My mate talked "pot odds" and could win off nothing—often when he was down to his last chips after a desultory night, and with whatever cards he had. Within the space of minutes, he had often won big, and had recovered handsomely. We wondered what he was financed back in the house, and several players deemed it wise to hide their winnings from their wives. I kept my face as suitably poker-like as I could and crawled into bed late with my meagre winnings.

CHAPTER 41 LITTLE NIPPERS

At the Summer Olympic Games, the Australians could be guaranteed to clean up in the pool. I had seen the Aussies go head-to-head with the Americans since I had watched the 1984 Los Angeles games as a boy, keeping the age-old rivalry alive.

In 2000, we had watched the freak Ian Thorpe with flipper-sized feet shatter records. In the Commonwealth games, Australia had been unbeatable in the medal tallies, big fish in an even smaller pond. The squad had time to extract themselves from medal ceremonies to turn up for the relays which they also won. It looked like the Institute of Sport bred freestyle and breaststroke specialists in test tubes, and new names were on hand to backfill spots vacated by those who'd conquered all.

No wonder the kids could swim by the time they started kinder.

"My kids will swim properly!" announced Kiki with a grim set to her face.

I stretched, and grimaced as she had a point. "Twist the knife!"

She had caught the sight of me swimming, and my faux-Tarzan effort of a lot of splashing, little progress, even, was not a good example. I admitted I could be a disaster in the water.

Even if you weren't into sea-swimming, we could use plenty of public baths. We had a guy at work who, at lunch, popped to the Melbourne Aquatic Centre MSAC around the corner for a swim—when he wasn't competing in triathlons.

Kiki said, "So. Let's take the kids to Surf Lifesaving lessons."

They had been to the pool but never to a beach to swim. "Sounds good, let's start next week."

It was on for young and old.

Most beaches on Bayside (the section of coast just down from the city) ran Surf Rescue Lifesaving Clubs manned by volunteers. They patrolled the sands from the clubhouse in their distinctive orange and yellow hats. Many clubs ran a "Little Nippers" section for the young 'uns to consolidate their swimming and learn the basics of surf rescue. It promoted safety too.

We chose Beaumaris Surf Lifesaving Rescue Club (SRLC) at Rickett's Point. It was a fabulous beach characterised by a rocky, scree section of rock pools at the top. Younger families spent an age looking for shells and crabs hopping gingerly over the rocks.

The kids gained in confidence in the sessions run by the club instructors, volunteer Mums and Dads. I loved seeing them sprint down the sands into the water with their boards under an arm. The instructors ran competitions involving a run along the beach, out to a rescue point in the surf, across the shoreline and back again. Kiki and I leant back on our elbows under our beach umbrella and watched their progression. At session's end, they marched up the sands and put away their equipment. There was almost a military aspect to it.

***

A life on the water was in demand. A mate, he of the poker, wanted to go fishing and found opportunities to explore Westernport when he could. He didn't plane the Bay but chose the less glamorous back bay. He motored out in a tinny (dinghy) towards French Island to secret spots he had scored.

He rung me once. "Come out tomorrow at five am."
I felt nothing but gratitude to be frank. I had taken Master Ten fishing, the father and son team we were, and not had much luck. The first mistake we made was fishing off the pier at Corinella. Tiny little toadfish ("toadies") nibbled the bait off the hook in seconds, so we gave up. We had better luck casting off the beach at Lang Lang, pitching our tent on the foreshore. The boy sent his hook whizzing out into the surf with a flick off the wrist and landed a few.

My mate and I headed out on a cold May morning, for a run

down to the coast which took half an hour at that deathly hour. We were on the water by 5:30 am. I don't know if it's true that it's coldest just after dawn, but we reached a new understanding of cold that day. Several sweatshirts under a lifejacket didn't quite cut it. We were lucky we had no wind as we'd be wracked with exhaustion just shivering. At first light, we were greeted with the sight of mist on the shore and the sky a vivid orange. The sun came up, and we admired that the surface of the water had taken on the appearance of a millpond.

Four of us headed out once, and we found it tough going, all trying to fit in the boat. The last thing we needed was a hook lodged in someone's face.

Having decided he wanted to take fishing seriously, the friend splashed out a lot of *coin* and upgraded to a bigger boat with a cabin. We could now push past the shelter of French Island into deeper waters. If nothing else, it was more comfortable, as we didn't have to deal with the rolling sides of a tinny or get splashed with salt-water.

We chased sleek and handsome Whiting, Flathead ("good eating"), Snapper and even gummy shark. Once we caught an Elephant fish—and found we had landed what you might expect to see if you crossed the Elephant Man with a fish. The clue was in the name. Dome-headed snapper came in season from spring until before Christmas, and enticed thousands, and even the lazy might accept an invitation to head out. I knew the smaller young were called "Pinkies" and my friend chucked these back if under-sized. Not all fish was tolerable in his opinion: Baracouda, not Barracuda, were only good for baitfish as they were so oily.

We saved the biggest fun for launching from Welshpool further along the coast, several hours drive past Phillip Island. He could ramp up the difficulty, and we could handle rougher seas. If Christ persuaded fisherman to cast off their nets for a higher calling, our own saviour called on us to take a day of leave to come out with him for his own rapture. We considered ourselves the chosen ones. It felt good to get out of the office to motor out further, and those of us with meetings found the 4G reception allowed a critical call.

In those depths, we chased Kingfish and bigger species in larger swell and beefed up the fishing line and weights accordingly.

I liked seeing the coastlines around Melbourne and surrounds. You didn't need to drive the north-west coast of Australia in Western Australia to places like Coral Bay to find magic. You could visit back beaches on the peninsula and have the beach to yourself on a Sunday afternoon.

A location that scored highly was about three hours south-east of Melbourne. It was the "Prom", or Wilson's Prom. It was a spit of land like Melbourne's own peninsula, which captured the imagination of every Victorian.

It is the most southerly location on the Australian mainland. It was the stuff of dreams and fantasies. At its tip, a lighthouse maintained a watch over the ocean. Remote destinations were days walk out from the car park. It proved so popular that many of its campsites fill at high season at Christmas and Easter, and people cast ballots to land scarce sites.

Kiki and I drove down there for a weekend break. We found the path to Squeaky Beach and took our trainers and socks off. Someone named it aptly of course, as the sands did indeed squeak like hell as we traipsed on them barefoot. We looked out to the sea and marvelled we had the place to ourselves. Our kids also camped there under the tutelage of their teachers who sent back photos. I found it enchanting from the clifftop to see the orderly line of tents laid out on the shore without a cloud in the sky, and the kids resembled ants. They surfed, water-skied, and toasted marshmallows by a fire. It was a rite of passage.

CHAPTER 42 ...AND LITTLE MITES

On a spring day we had been out on the deck before the mosquitoes arrived, appreciating the still of the evening. The breeze brought the occasional cry of laughter from across the fence from houses across the slope, but it was quiet. We felt the distinct humidity in the air, the first such evening.

Kiki announced, her voice full of wonder. "What are *they*?"

I looked around to follow her finger.

She pointed out flying and swarming ants, fluttering on the breeze. Where had they come from? They were everywhere, even wriggling in the fly screens. We had no idea what they were, locusts; ants, mini flying-cockroaches?

They were indeed ants, but "white ants" which meant one thing. Termites.

Termites were not unique to Australia, but we had never seen them in Europe. You heard about them getting into people's houses. It baffled me that houses were constructed out of wood framing. Apparently, they were everywhere. Tree stumps were full of them, as were old garden beds and fence posts. They chomped through wood and cellulose; including your immaculate and complete antique book collection—*War and Peace Unabridged* maybe, or your wall studs.

They formed nests with a queen, and it was the *workers* that chomped through your house. They were insidious little things and worked quietly hidden from sight. Ventilation and light were their enemies. The species in the tropics were speedsters. Apparently, you could almost hear them devouring your house at night.

One day, we noticed the floorboards in the dining room were uneven and the joins between the panels were damaged, even blistered. The first thing I suspected: subterranean termites.

We had the local pest control company over, and they didn't even look under the house. One worker punctured the floor blistering and found a lone termite which he squished under his thumb.

"Termites," he said. "Get it sorted."

The termite inspector arrived to have a look. He was an eccentric fellow and lived in the valley to the south-east. He shuffled through the house with a stick with a rubber ball attached, tapping away on boards, architraves, skirting boards, looking in the wardrobes. He looked a little crazy and peered around around myopically. He joined me for a cup of tea and gazed down the block. He answered a lot of my questions and dispelled a few fears.

A termite didn't just alight on your deck or on a piece of favourite outdoor setting—a lounge suite from Fantastic Furniture and start chomping—it required a colony to grow.

"Many don't survive without a source of food or moisture, though, Steve," he added. "They desiccate quickly."

The worker ants chomped their way through the wood, passing food and moisture back to the nest.

It seemed a little reassuring not every *white ant* we saw was traipsing through our floor space looking for fine-dining. He could treat the infestation, but we also needed to repair the damage. He left me at my desk with several browser tabs open on my screen. My time on Google was not wasted, and I became an expert on the matter almost overnight.

The builder we had engaged came and had a look. He drove a Nissan Navara ute and had the patience to do the jobs other tradies might turn their noses up at.

He scratched his head and thought about it. "If the termites are in the stud frame, and the walls, it's a matter of time before they hit the roof." He looked at me in a funny way.

I got the point. Presumably, our roof would collapse around us. As we were renovating the fireplace, the internal gyprock wall was going, anyway. He might as well look.

I came home from work to find neat holes in the wall and scrawled notes in felt-tip. He had left arrows pointing to the termite damage in the stud frames.

HERE > < HERE

We knew we had to get the flooring up and replace the studs too. I agonised about the roof.

I felt beyond peeved the termites had chosen *us*.

We paid a tidy sum for the treatment: $2,000. The pest inspector came back to treat the infestation, joined by two young offsiders. One dug trenches all around the foundations of the house and filled them with a potent treatment. It looked tricky working in the dark under there, and I didn't envy him. With a canister they wore knapsack-style, they injected tree stumps and likely places. They found a nest in a tree out the front and blitzed it. I jumped for joy.

The builder had the pine flooring up, and I looked into the cavity of the floor space. A termite tunnel led from the ground to the wall. The beasts had crawled around out of sight having the time of their lives.

"You're lucky they didn't get into the top plate," said the builder.

"Right," I volunteered.

That was something to be happy about. He meant the frame running atop the wall under the roof space. It'd be fiddly replacing that.

As it was, he came back with props to hold up our roof whilst he replaced the damaged studs, one at a time. We made sure to not be home that day. I am not sure I could have looked as the weight of one side of the house was taken on his props. That had to be a win—but the builder also dropped oil on the floor which dried and left a residue right next to the sofa. It was the final nuisance after all we had gone through.

CHAPTER 43 A PLACE TO CALL MY OWN

My world was simultaneously shrinking and expanding. Down the hill at the shops, developers had been going gangbusters, and shops were opening on the highway. Woolworths opened in the sleepy parade of shops, and we rejoiced we could do a big food shop without stopping at a red light.

More cafes opened to appeal to an early morning crowd and created competition. The lines of people queuing at hole-in-the-wall coffee shops increased as the South East grew. The Mexican restaurant went up in smoke one night. It had started in the antique shop next door: was this a nefarious stock take, the owner bailing out? Our sister fire brigade was busy that night.

Work was also expanding in the sense that it was taking over. Meetings, projects, these all expanded to fit. With growing children all past crawling, and in and out of kinder, or school, we had less space to study, pay a bill or even retreat to think.

Our little house had people allocated to every bedroom, the girls in one, Master Three in the other. We couldn't provision a bedroom for a back study, and sometimes the lazy option of a laptop in front of the TV didn't work out either. It was great to keep up with Netflix, but not great for finishing work.

I really wanted an office. A place of my own.

I looked down the block to the tree line and scratched my head. I wondered if I could build an office there. How would I make tea and coffee when the whim took me? I'd have to walk up and downhill a full 40 *metres* and get electricity put in.

I found a book about a US man who had built a little retreat on his rural property. He had engineered an office to the n'th degree. It was the height of sophistication. He had indulged in a lot of navel-gazing and worry, though, and I could see he had spent a fortune. I didn't need that though, I just needed a room. Then it hit me as I made a coffee in the kitchen. My gaze fixed on the space between the deck and the fence. There was enough of a gap for an office.

Chris said he'd help, and would come by on the weekend. We needed to build the foundations and frame it up.

"What you need, mate, is stumps," he said.

"Great, I'll help you with the concrete mixing," I replied.

He arrived on Saturday with bags of sand, cement, and a tray of gravel. I retrieved my wheelbarrow and wheeled the bags down the side. Mixing in water, and aggregate, we mixed up concrete in a slurry until we had the right consistency.

A quick inspection at the site where the office would go was in order. The ground comprised of pavers, level enough. I had some bricks under the deck, and it didn't take long to ferry them over. We created stumps with these, in Lego-like fashion held with the cement slurry.

"Time for breakfast, mate," I said.

"Sounds good," he replied, wiping his hands on his knees.

We retired to the kitchen, and I fried bacon and eggs in a hot pan. My helper looked at me in consternation. "For Christ's sake, cut the fat off the bacon, and, I need it *crispy*," he said.

"Ok, mate." I was so happy to have his help, I'd comply with any diet request.

"I once almost choked on bacon, it terrifies me." The haunted look on his face said it all.

I excused myself from proceedings, and popped out to the fire station for our monthly meeting. A rumour had flown around one of our lieutenants had a problem with our captain. When called on to provide his report, the "lieuy" remained seated and read from a script he had prepared.

"Ah…" he started.

Brigade members looked up, and he continued. "I can't carry on working with the captain. That's all there is to it."

Our captain normally adopted a jovial expression, even

running to a twinkle in his eye, but this faded when he realised the report was a slight on the way he ran the brigade. What had been private between them was about to become public. This came out as the lieutenant laboured over his message, his reading glasses perched on the bridge of his nose. People with blank faces took on quizzical looks, and bored members became interested.

"After all the infighting and disagreement, I have no choice." It looked like the lieutenant was summing up. "With immediate effect, I'm resigning from First Lieutenant."

He finished reading as a silence fell on the room. He removed his glasses, stood up, and headed to the kitchen to fetch a cup of tea.

We didn't even know half the story. But, the curious thing was that most people in the brigade cheered his departure. It was just one of those things. Not everyone got on, and not everything worked out.

We made the office floor next. We did this by framing up pine in a lattice, and nailing yellow tongue boards across. Now we had a floor with a gap under for airflow (and rats, presumably.) It reminded me of a dais for the performing arts.

The fun part was framing the sides. As if we were building a house, we planned a stud frame every half a metre. We used a nail gun and compressor, powering in nails to affix each join securely. It felt great as the nail punched in. Next, we added a skillion roof; a flat one—a slanting one—so rainwater would run off. The cladding went on next, baltic pine boards to beautify the exterior, and the windows went in the next day.

I now had a clad office with a metal roof and a door, and windows to see out. It was basic, but fit for purpose. Chris, his pencil behind his ear, looked pleased and smiled, his curls hanging down.

***

"Do you know what I am going to do for your birthday?" Kiki

said. "I'm finishing the office so it will look a million dollars."

The office was useable, and I'd hide in there one day a week to work from home. It was a bit warm in there, and it was not very glam. I came back from the city one day to find serious "work in progress" by a local builder.

Soon it was done. He had run merbau feature panelling under the roofline. I could see gutters, and eaves incorporating down lights for exterior lighting under the fascia. A varnished door hung, a key in the lock ready to go. Also inside, a decent floor of Tasmanian oak, adding warmth, and they had added interior walls and skirting boards.

After adding a partner's desk and a chair, and table lamps, I was all ready to go.

I had at last got my space. I liked having an acre of land, even if half of it was down the back in bushland. I felt I needed to use it. Woodworking seemed a good idea. I set up a saw table and router in my garage and with the back door open for ventilation and light, I set to work. My creations were both ridiculous and modest, a tiny little table for Miss Two, and a chair.

I searched the timber yards and found Blackwood and Bluegum immeasurably attractive to work in. The smell of the sawn wood was incredible, but the potting and planting table Kiki asked me to make never saw the light of day. I foud it hard when a nappy needed changing, or an errand run.

In the end, I accepted I was merely a dilettante.

CHAPTER 44 ALL'S FAIR IN LOVE AND SPORT

We had a sporting superstar in our midst. The rugby Full Back and TV sensation Billy Slater moved to a palatial house across the valley from us, and moved his horses up. It looked like he might be branching out into polo. Friends bumped into him in the milk bar and noted he had looked pretty normal. Rugby League was popular in Sydney with a large competition, but he played for the team in Melbourne called the Storm which we had got to occasionally, shouting ourselves hoarse.

On TV, I'd watched the southern-hemisphere giants of New Zealand, South Africa and Australia lock horns. In 1999, Australia won the World Cup for the second time. When I arrived in Sydney, in 2002, I itched to get my hands on a rugby ball.

Imagine my surprise then, when I realised Rugby Union was a minority game after Australian Rules Football, Rugby League. But meanwhile, if Victorians played Australians Rules, *that* was the game I'd take my boy to.

It was weird seeing him play. He played a game I had little skill in and used ball skills I never picked up. He came home from primary school with the ability to bounce the ball along the ground every few steps back into his hand without losing it sideways. You need to be brought up doing this, as it doesn't come easily, and I tried. He started out in Auskick, a programme that prepared young boys for playing the big game. The tackling wasn't so hard, and they kept the rules simple. At 11, they were playing the full length of the pitch.

Fathers told me he played OK in midfield, in the half-back line. It was a proud moment when he was awarded the Coach's Award the year he turned 13. Each season, the coaching staff award "Best and Fairest" to a player based on votes every week. It rewards the player who runs a tight game but upholds sportsmanship. The "Coach's Award" is given to the player who shows flair and grit. Coach made a speech about Master Twelve.

"This player was one of the first boys I noticed when I took over the side. I even sent my runner on to the pitch to find out who this boy was, I didn't know his name."

To me, that said it all. There might have been a bit of dust in the room because it sure got into my eye.

Meanwhile, my daughters had both been bitten by the dance bug and were dancing after school in a local studio. Dance was very competitive, not just an art form but a hyperactive whirlwind of "*comps*"—competitions—and travel. The girls endured early starts, hours of makeup, and their emotions ran high; their mother was in the thick of it! They started out in general categories then moved up to the "Industry" grade where the angst and the stakes loomed higher again. I worried about the pressure to be honest, but they seemed to flourish in it.

My youngest girl was very technical and worked hard. She asked me to take her to a solo competition. I sat as an ignorant outsider at the back and watched as she pirouetted on the stage and executed her moves in the limelight. She placed first out of fourteen girls, and when we showed her mother the rosette, Kiki looked at her as if she had known all along.

CHAPTER 45 SOLAR

"Steve, the electricity bill is on the steep side," Kiki said. She dangled the offending article in her hand whilst I sat at the kitchen table minding my own business—which wasn't paying bills.

"How much?" I asked.

"Four-hundred dollars for the quarter. And it's going to get a lot worse."

"Maybe it's time to install solar," I replied.

I felt confident about this, as installs were on the rise.

When we first arrived, new houses were installing solar panels for hot water systems, part of the sign-off they need for a "5 star" energy home rating. I thought it a no-brainer of course. After all, we lived in a country renowned for sunshine. European countries like Germany were light-years ahead. Perhaps Australians were slower than they might have been in installing rooftop systems.

The upfront of the install was subsidised by a government scheme. A typical install ran about $10,000, using Australian panels or a European invertor. If you used Chinese parts, you paid less again.

Kiki continued. "We can use this solar, Steve, for the washing machine and the dishwasher. The thing is," she said, "we are out of the house during the day when the sun is up. The power is not being used."

"We'd need a battery. But they are not up to it, yet," I replied.

If we could not store the power, it was no use at night when we needed it—for the dishwashers and heating, let alone lighting. Batteries in cars were renowned to be near impossible to replace economically. If I had little trust the battery in my cordless drill held a charge after a year or two, what about a solar install?

I searched it up on Google.

"The electricity companies make it viable by paying you for the unused generated power you push back to the grid."

It was wise to *not* use it.

"It's called a PFIT—a Premium Feed-In Tariff," I read out from a website I'd found.

This premium had to be quite the incentive. The power companies didn't just pay you for a kilowatt of energy. If a kilowatt cost ten cents an hour, to make it worth your while, they paid a whopping 66 cents. What's more, the scheme ran until 2024. This guaranteed for many the payoff came soon. In fact, scores of people raced to get in and added 3-5kW systems on farm sheds with no intention of using any solar-generated power. Their intention—to bank the money and run. It made sense to install the largest system you could.

But the scheme deadline was running out, and we had to be installed and signed off by September.

"Let's whack it on the mortgage," I said.

Even if we paid interest on it over the longer term, we'd still be better off cash flow-wise month to month.

A bloke from a local company came out and sat in the same armchair the mortgage guy had sat in, only the chair had worn now. He had a MacBook in his lap and looked our house up on what looked like Google Earth to see which way it ran. His idea: we needed to use the north-facing roof.

"It's not Google Earth," he said, as I craned forward to look. "This is software I have access to."

He plugged away at it and soon had a recommendation for us.

"A three-kilowatt system will fit. No dramas."

We had roofline to add north-facing panels to catch the sun as it arced over, and we added other panels to catch the morning sun.

They installed the system in a day. To be honest, the crew made it look easy as they attached the panels to the roof. The challenge now—to get *it signed off*. That's what worried me. We could do all the work on the install, but if we didn't get certified by the due date, the contract wouldn't count, and we'd lose those 66 cents. I was nervous. We may have had weeks to spare but the installer couldn't say with any certainty when the inspector might arrive.

"I booked you in at two pm," said my provider over the phone. "He's pretty good."

"What day are we looking at?" I asked.

"Er, the seventeenth," he replied.

I knew that as the last day of the programme.

"Hope he's not late," I replied. Now I felt terrified. The provider said nothing. It was not his problem, now, and I eyed him as warily as you can eye someone when that person is on the end of a line.

***

At 1 pm, on the last day, a white ute arrived in the driveway.

"It's ten minutes to midnight, isn't it?" said a gentleman, stepping out of his cab. He wore a pair of RM Williams and held a clipboard in his hand.

"It certainly is," I said.

I could have kissed him.

Of course, as soon as the scheme ended, the cost of the install dropped to encourage take-up. Still, we thought we were doing our bit for the environment, and we saved a lot of money.

We did well, but others had sorrier stories to tell. Power companies didn't automatically give you the 66 cents, you had to apply for it. Chris came to the fenceline to crow about his massive system.

He said, "I commissioned my five-kilowatt install. It's in."

Quick as a flash, I replied. "Did you apply for the sixty-six cents?"

"Eh?"

"You have to talk to your retail company before the deadline, mate."

His face fell about a yard when he realised his error.

His hoped-for 66 cents plummeted to 18 cents, and in later years, this fell to a miserly six cents. Still, solar systems went from being cash cows to blunting the trauma households faced when they got their bills.

CHAPTER 46 THE ALPINE

We lived twenty minutes from the Dandenong ranges. If we headed due north, we could be at Mount Dandenong. But we knew of higher, more adventurous country to see. The hills were only the beginning.

The Great Dividing Range extends from west of Melbourne well into Queensland, passing through New South Wales. The Macedon ranges rise to the north-west of the city, which I drove through one summer. The weather was different across the divide there. I was amazed to leave a cool day in Melbourne to find it warm *across the divide*. I thought it an oddity.

To the north-*east*, you ascended the range through old forestry above Healesville on the highway across a spur called "Black Spur"—you wound along the road for a good half-hour until you got to a pub at the top. The trees rose fifty meters, and outsized ferns leered over the road. We expected a T-Rex to part the bushes and stick out an angry head any moment. The weather changed too, with the altitude. Coming back to Melbourne, I have often descended from fresh blue skies to less agreeable city mist and seen the car temperature gauge drop.

The Dividing Range culminates in a series of mountains, many over 1,500 metres high. Whilst they have nothing on the high French ski resorts at 3,000-4,000 metres or even Mont Blanc (5,000 metres) this is still twice the height of Mt Snowdon in Wales.

Mount Feathertop, the "Queen of the Victorian Alps", is 2,000 metres high, and is a classically formed jagged mountain peak. The highest is Mt Bogong, not as alluring as a destination—flatter and less adventurous. Over in New South, the peaks are called the "Main Range", and they are higher still.

We ascended as summer bushwalkers and walked to Craig's Hut. This is a location made famous by the 1978 movie *The Man*

From Snowy River. Many people drive it in a 4x4, have lunch, and barely break a sweat. The hut looked worse for wear and falling apart, but it burnt down in 2007 and they rebuilt. A friend twisted his ankle, and it took an age to walk out with him limping along stoically.

An entire culture and mystique surrounded the High Country. Like the United States West, I found it enjoyed a "frontier" type culture and history. In the nineteenth century, people walked and explored the flats and rivers, and the peaks. People were murdered or went missing—the whole slice and dice, and intrigue. People had gone missing recently, too. I watched a TV documentary which counted all the people that had gone missing just in the last few years and I changed the channel not wishing to scare the kids.

Men and women bought 4x4 cars and trucks and headed off to campsites, many of which were remote. We are not talking Canadian wilderness, but help could be the best part of a day away if you were immobilised—a snake bite, say.

Lying between the ski resorts in the north, and the beach towns of Gippsland is a wilderness called the Avon. Part of this is dedicated to the Alpine National Park. Mountains soar to 1,700 metres high—above the snowline—and in the valley, large river systems like the Moroka river careen over rocks and loamy banks. These attract hikers who love to float along the river on inflatable rafts.

You can hunt and shoot in the Alpine Park, so it is not unusual to hear a gunshot when camping which amazed me and made hiking in the UK seem literally like a walk in the park. The law had something to say though. A rifle can't be carried loaded on a footpath or discharged across a track or road. No one can hunt at night, or with a spotlight, but the police pick up plenty of idiots who try. The reality is the hunters are well off the main tracks.

Wildfires blazed for days, and the CFA brought in helicopters to attack remote fire. In the summer of 2006-2007, fire tore through 4,000 acres across the Divide. When vegetation grows back, termed "regrowth"—paths well-travelled become overgrown. The guidebooks that describe popular routes to beauty spots were rendered useless. I found it difficult that much-loved places were out of action for so long. And if it wasn't fire, it was landslides caused by torrential rainfall.

I thought I might apply for the "Hover Exit" job where the CFA dropped you off on foot. I was fit, could cover ground, and read a map. I had proven I could work at heights and follow instruction under pressure. But I'd start at the bottom again, and I rued it wouldn't pay well. Besides, I had that mortgage to knock over.

CHAPTER 47 INTO THE GREAT WIDE OPEN

A favourite place for us was a set of campsites along the Wellington River as it followed the tarmacadam road out of Licola in the south-west of the area. There were 14 in number, and you took your pick. Many had a warren of tracks that led to the river. It was first-come, first-served, and during the Christmas holidays every turnout and site along the tracks was full. You felt you were in the middle of nowhere, but you were only 20 minutes from the small town of Licola where you could refuel and buy a coffee. At the General Store, I found a copy of *Wildlife of the Snow Country* which enthralled me with loads of photos.

I took my son there once when he was seven years old. We met friends and set up by the river. The boys waded in the river or floated on their backs on a lilo, whatever took their fancy; providing they didn't crack a head on a half-submerged rock.

Kiki talked about the time she once slept like a baby under a full moon, on a clear night, her hair like tentacles across her eyes. The weather was so good, all she did was set her sleeping bag on a blowup mat. It was late in April, and we had the site to ourselves. After Easter, the sites are the preserve of walkers and hunters who huddle over a fire to ward off the chill of the autumn evenings.

Once we took our Ford sedan gingerly along the dirt track 30 kilometres into the Alpine Park. Our goal was a lake called Tali Karng deep in the bush. We knew it would be several hours walk, half of it switch-backing down a 20-degree slope, grabbing hold of bushes and kicking footholds in between tree roots.

The trees at the lake seemed impenetrable. The level of the lake varied based on recent rainfall, but it was fifty metres deep, like a miniature Russian Lake Baikal. When we visited, the water was high—but low enough to stand on an uncovered shore and look across the aquamarine surface to the forest on the other shore. We didn't see another person the whole trip. Kiki took off her boots and socks and dipped a toe in.

"It's freezing cold!" she said.

"What's wrong with your toes?"

She shrugged. "Blisters. But they'll be alright."

We spent awhile gazing around, contemplating the climb back up. We took the Echo track which meandered to the top. Some people find heading down hard on the knees, but we puffed all the way up.

We lit a fire to keep warm and sat there, looking at the stars. Indigenous peoples laugh at people who light huge fires and see these as "white man" efforts. I also preferred a small one arranged like a star, feeding the wood in, bit by bit. Then we crawled into our tent once it had burnt low.

On the way back next day, within striking distance of the car, Kiki stopped.

She said, "I've got sore feet. My toes have been hitting the front of my boots!"

She put on a brave face and overtook me. She upped the pace, and we sped-marched to the car, me trailing behind as rear-guard. She obviously had enough for now and wanted to get back as soon as possible. I was pleased she had come with me and gave it her all, and that we hadn't been seen off by the snakes.

Wildlife of the Snow Country from the store described the snakes that inhabit the High Country, interesting when I was safe and sound at home in my armchair; but walkers are nervous about meeting one in summer when they are active.

I once walked up Mount Tamboritha as a sole hiker on a February day, the last month of summer—conscious of every step I took, looking at the track. Right up until my concentration lapsed. I knew my mind had wandered when I felt a movement on the track. Instinctively, I leapt a foot in the air and landed near a snake which had scurried away. It frightened the wits out of me.

Remembering all snakes in Victoria are venomous, I was in no doubt this was a Tiger. How did I know? It blocked the path and stared me down, and the stripes were a giveaway. I retreated slowly, not wanting to take my eyes off it. Even a few chance stones and twigs thrown its way did not dislodge it from its ensconced position, and so we found ourselves in a standoff lasting five minutes, although it seemed like an age. I didn't like its evil eye. I wore gaiters, carried a PLB and a snake bandage, but I was correct to act wary. If I got bitten, I knew to lie still and activate my beacon. To move around would only hasten the venom through my lymphatic system.

CHAPTER 48 MATE'S TRIPS

One night I camped with my mates, and the temperature plummeted, and we woke to find our tents with a layer of frost on the flysheets. We thought the campsite was a *corker*, a great one, and we brought our kids here many a time to swim in the river and to toast marshmallows over an open fire. It poured with rain at breakfast, and we cowered under the cover of the tourist information display whilst the shower passed over.

The Great Ocean Road is placed high on any tourist's list of things to do when they visit. It is Australia (or Victoria's) answer to the US's Pacific Highway in California. Operators run minibuses along its length which stretches from Torquay in the east to Port Campbell in the west.

The standout is the Twelve Apostles, a collection of rock outcrops in the Southern Ocean which you can view from the clifftops, or even from the beach via a tourist centre, underground. Helicopter companies will fly you over the area, but they stop short of landing you on the rocks or strafe-bombing the locals. Another rock formation is called London Bridge, and I suppose it looked like the famous namesake. It was connected to the mainland until 1990, when part of it collapsed leaving a couple stranded for a bit and the news made the world news.

One day I opened the *Herald Sun* to find another tragedy.

"You're not going to believe this..." I said, showing Kiki the paper.

An Apostle had fallen into the sea, leaving eleven. Erosion does that, in a display of nature at its best. The Twelve were no more. This did nothing to deter the flocks of tourists that flock there and they kept coming. What is less known though, is the hinterland along those majestic cliffs. A walk opened in the mid-2000s, and we walked a section one summer.

We boys had the idea we would walk from Aire River to Wreck Beach, walking east to west with the sun behind us. The route led out through cliff-top meadows, and on to the beaches with the tide in or out. Part of this took us along twisty roads through eucalypt forests.

We had planned three nights, just long enough to make it feel like it wasn't a weekend nor a week; short enough if we got wet, or had blisters, there might be only one last day to endure. Overall, a Goldilocks trip. We took two cars to the end and dropped mine for the return trip, and took one back to the start.

I thought it the kind of military *"Pre-positioning"* you saw on Antarctic trips.

We were as well prepared as we could be. We had worked out after other trips we needed the lightest packs possible. As middle-aged blokes, we deserved to give our bodies the benefit of the doubt. The goal: to carry about 10 kilogrammes each. I had a 50-litre pack, and a down sleeping bag which packed to the size of a milk carton.

"Inspector Gadget!" someone said.

Apart from a tent, I carried a litre of water, and food I could add water to, rather than tins. I packed a head torch, penknife, and a few band aids and pills. I took a spare t-shirt, a warm jacket for in-camp, spare socks and underwear. Any fool can be uncomfortable, but excess weight makes anyone miserable.

We marvelled at each other's gear and swapped notes. We ran little spreadsheets and calculated what our packs might weigh on Day One. The packs always ended up heavier than planned, though. I could only guess a little fairy, imp, or *petite malin* had hidden a small, invisible rock in the bottom. One of our number turned up with a cheap pack.

"Just to test it," he pointed out.

Much of the route snaked along clifftops with the ocean to our left. This came as no surprise—the clue was in the name. We had the route to ourselves most of the time, but an occasional walker or even cyclist approached and waved as they shot past. Our route petered down through grass tussocks then scree, and took us to the ocean's edge.

We found ourselves on a beach divided by rocks. The way to get to the end was to clamber over the rocks as the incoming tide came in, timing our crossing when the sea rested between surges. We went for it one at a time, and I got caught by a surge as I triumphantly leapt to dry rock.

Our feet stayed wet the rest of the day, and I was well pleased to get my spare socks out the next morning until they got damp too. Our boots did not dry out over night as we had hoped. We overnighted in a lightly treed area and shared it with another hiker. He had rigged a small Australian Army tarp in Auscam camouflage between trees. It rained after we put our tents up, and when I looked out, he'd adjusted the tarp, so the rain didn't come in from the side. He seemed cheery enough, though, and nodded when I called "Good Morning."

On the second day, we sighted a yellow snake as we walked through the bush. It chose not to flee and eyed me warily as I clomped on through. I stopped to have a look and called out to the others.

"All Victorian snakes are venomous, chaps!" I declared. "Look at this guy!"

We eyed it until it took off.

For lunch, we stopped at a metal shelter, and finding the site convivial, rested for a few hours, enjoying the warmth of the sun as it passed overhead. It felt like we were at a disused bus stop long unserviced, but we knew the only transport was back on the track. Our friend with the trial pack had an equipment failure—his pack gave way and swung on a broken strap behind him. He fixed it with a safety pin, grinning inanely.

"How's that looking?" I asked, trying not to laugh.

"I need to get a decent pack." He shrugged. "As my Dad would say, it's a false economy skimping on gear." He grinned.

We felt sore on waking on the last day. My shoulders rubbed a smidge from my pack straps, a breeze fluttering the guy ropes and sending ripples through the flysheet. My back ached from a lump in the ground I hadn't spotted when picking a site for the tent.

We stood under the trees and brewed cups of tea or coffee on our little gas burners, their roar the only sound we heard apart from birdsong. Not much was said that morning. We knew we had the last day and the distance to come. We got through it and were pleased to finish.

We spent the last night in a caravan park, feeling pleased with our mini-achievement, and had a few stubbies. The wind picked up and blew as we considered the trip at a campsite table. I was glad of the rigger jacket I had packed, but a mate felt chilled in his cotton t-shirt, and he shivered without complaining. A reminder of the old maxim that "cotton kills".

We were all packed and squared away when I realised I couldn't locate my car key. A panicked search ensued, and I found it down the bottom of my sleeping bag. I was relieved to be spared further humiliation, of having to arrange alternate transport, or be marooned out here, but the others found it hilarious.

CHAPTER 49 BLACK SATURDAY

BLEEP! BLEEP! BLEEP! BLEEP!

What was that? I looked at where the noise was coming from. Of course—it was my pager; it could be nothing else. Miss Number Two came running with it and passed it over. Did Daddy have to head off to a fire?

I was up on a Saturday morning, early as always. Two little girls or a boy are bound to wake me on any day, and the weekend was no different. I squinted at the two-line display:

FIRE1 CODE1 GRASS1 Village Location. Grass and Scrub fire at 76 Ridge Road 280

It was a Code One callout which meant we could travel with lights, adding sirens as necessary. Like many a Total Fire Ban Day, it was already noticeably warm by 7 am. Overnight had not brought welcome relief or change. The heat would start heading up by 9 am, we knew that. When I walked on to the back deck, the other thing was the wind. It gusted often, sending the upper boughs and branches of the willow trees bending. Leaves lay tossed against the wire fence.

The drive to the fire took twenty minutes, as it was out of our patch. But with the Total Fire Ban Day, and the Fire Danger Index so high, we were responded too. It had been drilled into us a bushfire couldn't get out of control early. We had better nip it in the bud.

When we arrived, the paddock was alight—what we call a running grass fire. We attacked it the prescribed way, spraying from the "ROPS" (Roll Over Protection System) as the driver followed the fire front. The last thing we needed was the tyres of our truck melting. We were incredulous when we found out how the fire had started. The property owner had been using an angle-grinder, and he would have known. It was not hot yet, but we were already warm in our "yellows". We were glad to be out earlier in the day, but who knows what the afternoon would bring?

We returned to the fire station relieved it was not a big a deal, and awaited developments as the temperatures climbed after lunch. We warily knew temps would peak at teatime. Meanwhile, the locals were playing it safe—no one had done anything silly, nor lit a fire in the open, nor sighted smoke. I wondered if the dangerous day would end on a positive note.

My captain approached me.

"Join me for a drive around, Steve."

We sped around in the fire utility in the afternoon checking for embers or smoke. We saw nothing but quiet. Everyone sat it out at home watching TV.

Nothing happened of any note until someone turned on the TV to channel Seven.

We expected the live feed of small fires and incidents across the metro area and footage of the aerial firefighting helicopters and airframes hitting outbreaks. We got far worse. The news anchor barely concealing his excitement reported that a major fire raged north-east of Melbourne. An enormous fire front had approached the city and had gone through small townships and villages an hour away.

I'll never forget the words I heard.

"Marysville has gone," someone said. "There's nothing left."

Marysville.

A summer spot famous for day-trippers out of Melbourne, for coffee, pies, and brunch. I had never been, but people raved about it. It was not far away from the ski resort of Lake Mountain. People were losing their lives not that far away.

Whilst we sat with little to do in the fire station, villages 25 miles (40km) as the crow flies to our north were burning. We watched as it unfolded on the television coverage. We were cool in the air-conditioning of the station, but it hit a never seen 46 degrees in the early afternoon and peaked at 48. At that point, Melbourne was one of the hottest places on earth, easily achieved when you consider most of the world slept in the depths of winter.

We got responded again.

The captain came into the watch room. "Guys. That fire we put out this morning has lit back up and is threatening homes across the back road in Nanadoon."

"He's an idiot!" someone said.

The homeowner had gone back out to finish his DIY and had once more set fire to his paddock. The out-of-control fire leapt across the road and was heading towards houses. It was the village I had stayed in when I first arrived in Melbourne.

The captain dispatched one of our tankers and a crew to the scene choosing those who had not gone in the morning, which left me and others in the fire station watching the news on TV. Later, they come back exhausted having been through the ringer. One firie had almost gone down with heat exhaustion and had to lie in the shade under a tree. Later we counted the cost—several houses destroyed, more damaged, but no loss of life to people or animals.

"The police are going to throw the book at him," the captain said. "You just can't do that on a day like this. It's criminal."

The warning had gone out the day before. The Bureau of Meteorology had forecast a scorcher of a day. The BOM got it right—if they say it's going to be *hot*, they are not wrong. The Premier appeared on TV, too, and told us it would be bad. Those were his exact words. When fire broke out, the conditions spelt doom for many.

It was sobering the next day, Sunday, when the Melbourne media summarised the loss of life—220 people in several towns and villages, entire villages and townships wiped out. The smoke from the fires hung over the city for days. People gathered in kitchens in offices and shrugged. To many city dwellers, fire happened to people who chose to live in the country; their attitude: it was a self-inflicted situation. This day though joined the list of "bad days". Victoria had Black Saturday in 1939, then Ash Wednesday in 1983. This day in 2009 got called Black Saturday.

The util companies traced the source of the mega fire from the north to sparking fallen power cables brought down by wind. After various class actions, the companies are now far more proactive in maintaining power lines and cutting back vegetation. They are often out in our street with cherry pickers loping branches.

***

The local council asked us to attend awards at the civic centre where they awarded medals to thank us for our contribution. None of us considered ourselves to be worthy—it wasn't the George Medal or Military Cross. I walked to join my firie mates, and had to stop to grab my youngest girl, not even aged two who'd run off, and take her to receive my medal.

The next day at work in the kitchen, I bumped into a colleague as he took out his steaming lunch from the microwave and held it aloft.

"Steve. You're famous, mate."

I glanced at the *Herald Sun* he showed me back at his desk. There I was, on Page Three in full colour, clutching my youngest. At the café downstairs, I noticed the owners had Blu-Tacked the page above the counter with the words "A Hero Amongst Us". I thought it a splendid touch. I had unknowingly found myself a newspaper poster boy for the Country Fire Authority. The feat repeated next week, when I found myself accosted by a photographer and found myself in the *Pakenham Times*. Want to get in a newspaper? Just wear firefighters' gear and have a child accessory.

CHAPTER 50 WATER, WATER, EVERYWHERE

"**S**teve, we need rainwater tanks," Kiki said one morning. "We need to store rain and use it for washing. Look at the reservoir levels."

"If it doesn't rain, how can we catch it?" would have been a silly response.

"They are low," I said out loud.

She showed me the newspaper outlining the water restrictions Melbourne was heading for. After a hot summer, the reservoirs were at a new low. Saving water had to be a favourite topic amongst anyone who had a conscience.

We knew we had signed up to live in a hot country, but Australia had a history of drought which came and went over the decades. Our current drought had set in around 1996, and was referred to as the "Millennial" drought. Most of the southern tip of Australia was in its grip. Parts of the Peninsula had been the driest on record.

Dorothea Mackellar said it best in her 1906 epic poem *My Country*: when she talked about Australia being a land of both droughts and rains. Years of "The Dry" might break with a wet period, flooding low-lying plains and causing rivers to breach banks.

We were already on "Stage One Restrictions". The State government banned automatic water sprinklers. We could save our gardens and water by hand, and people rinsed cars with a high-pressure nozzle. To be honest, this wasn't the end of the world. Perhaps they could have gone harder sooner.

I said, "Luckily, the pool doesn't need topping up." I had reduced the evaporation with a solar blanket which also kept the water warmer.

Kki smiled. "It's good swimming to April."

People weren't listening, though, and stood there for an age watering their gardens, so now Stage Two was coming. We couldn't water our lawns at all. Many of us had hardy, warm-weather grasses like kikuyu which would survive the regime.

The calamity was there for all to see. Melbourne's water supplies had reached 25 per cent. Local people walking their dogs noticed the exposed banks of the reservoirs. The grass in the city was suffering and nature strips had turned to dust. To be honest, I found it depressing as I alighted the tram at Domain junction near work.

Installing rainwater tanks had to be one way of doing our bit.

"The thing is, there's a government grant we can use to offset the cost," Kiki continued.

"Go on," I replied. This sounded good.

"Well, I was thinking. Let's get water-saving loos, too."

Our current ones had a half-flush setting, like you found in continental Europe. But we could go one better; newer types used less water again.

Kiki called the local tank and irrigation supply companies and spoke to sales teams, making notes in her notebook. She went with a company on the Princes Highway in Officer.

"Here's the plan," she said. "Two tanks, a large one, and a small one. The small one will be 2,500 litres. We can put that on the side of the house by the pool."

"We can top the pool up, then?" I asked.

"Yes. I'm adding a tap for the garden, so we can attach a hose," she said. "The large tank will go the other side," she added.

"How big is the large one?" I asked.

Many people in the village had 9,000 litre tanks, two metres wide. For us, they were a smidge too wide, though, and we'd not fit past our decking. There was a 7,500 litre tank one and a half metres wide.

Kiki said, "The 7,500 litre tank will fit, I checked."

The tanks arrived on a truck and the workers manhandled the

smaller tank in through the garage. They craned the larger tank over the fence from next door. We made sure Chris had been tipped off.

We plumbed the larger tank into the loos, laundry tub and washing machine. It was nice using rainwater, but we needed to wash clothes and use the loo if we ever ran low, so the fitter added a fill facility from mains water. A bobbing float detected when the water level dipped and opened a valve for top up.

Two new china thrones went in next: they were adorned with five-star stickers extolling their thriftiness.

***

"Fifty bucks!" exclaimed Kiki when we received our next bill and danced a jig around the kitchen.

Over the quarter, our water use fell drastically. I don't think we ever got a bill higher than $50 for a while. We had done the right thing by the environment.

The State government was so appalled Melbourne had gone down to the wire, it built a desalination plant on the Peninsula, to drought-proof the water supply. It was done and dusted by 2012. I knew we needed to protect the water supply for generations to come. But why not just recycle the water like in Europe? By 2010-2011, we were out of drought in a *La Niña* year. Brisbane copped it badly, and suburbs on the river flooded.

Australia really was a land of extremes.

CHAPTER 51 A WEEK ON THE FARM

Years before, I had spent time on a sheep station after completing a week's training in Queensland. We were barely ready, but we were matched with employers and sent out on transport: by rail, coach, or even plane to get to jobs. My farm lay in Central West New South. It ran sheep on quad bikes.

I ended up helping with shearing one Easter: mustering, and dosing sheep. We looked after 4,000, collecting and organising them in pens ready to be brought into be shorn. Not quite all in a day's work, but more like a week.

I received a call from a friend in the village asking me if I'd like to go to the football with her husband and her parents who were down from New South. I met them at the local station and a man in his sixties approached me, smiling, as I parked up.

"That's a farmer's ute," he said, pointing at it.

I had to agree—it looked a bit ragged compared to the flash Toyotas the tradies had.

We got on like a house of fire. On the ride up to town, he told me about his farm near Wagga, north of the Hume highway in the centre of NSW. To my advantage, my daughter loved him and bounced up and down on his knee, much to his delight; he clearly loved children.

We spoke more as the train halted at the stops. In the same way my grandfather had been in the church and had been appointed a Canon of Christchurch, his own ancestors had been descendants of English Archbishops. They had singularly managed what my grandfather had failed to do.

He told me to come and visit and I thanked him, not sure if he meant it. He made good with this offer when he rang asking if I'd like to house-sit the property whilst they were in Thailand. I jumped at the chance and took a week off work.

***

I rose early and drove to New South Wales. I wasn't surprised to see that the grass was brown out in the regions. Last week, even the city looked dire, with sections of once green parkland in South Melbourne not only brown and desiccated, but barren dirt.

We had not long got back from the US and Europe, and it was sobering to see Melbourne so brown from the air when New Zealand across the ditch was so green.

My route took me alongside the Dandenongs to the east, alongside the Yarra Valley, past Healesville towards the country town of Yea. The roadsides were still parched and dry even in the shadow of the Dandenongs. Back routes cut across to Seymour, thence to the never-ending Hume highway. From there, I planned to cut across land to Wagga. I stopped in Yea and had an iced coffee; and a pie: it was a typical country town with an extra-wide street with a central reservation, with the servo at one end and a cop car with a speed camera at the other.

I crossed the border and noticed the change in number plates —and expected everyone to be dressed in Rugby League club colours rather than the customary Victorian Aussie Rules teams I'd got used to.

I broke the monotony of the Hume Highway and took a more direct route across country along straight back roads where I saw no one. Many Australian rural areas had such roads to get locals point to point. They ran as straight as the old Roman roads in the UK. This road left the road near Chiltern and through Lockhart. This country was flat, and the fields and paddocks dry. The occasional farm ute rushed past in the opposite direction.

The farm was up a road which snaked for 40 minutes from Wagga, so not outback, just in the regions. I had been told the homestead was visible from the road, and sure enough I saw. I swung in from the mailbox, noting the driveway was lined by plane trees, and took my time to become acquainted with the weatherboard property.

It felt satisfying to see no one, but I found two dogs in residence at the back who heard my ute crunch up. They didn't bark or yap: they seemed accustomed to strangers.

Looking around, the paddocks surrounding the property were dry as a bone, like the "Driz-a-bone" brand of lore—mostly flat. An interesting hill behind the property sloped to higher ground. In fact, the house hid at its base.

Next to the house, I looked at a metal grain silo near shedding, and what looked like a water tower. Closer inspection showed me this was diesel fuel with a delivery line, a good thousand litres. This far out of town it was better to buy it in from a tanker doing the rounds locally. There was a huge chicken shed, with elaborate fox-proofing, and amongst the shedding, a workshop.

The property was running beef. It was disappointing to see the farm stricken by the drought, with the grassless ground all around dry and firm. The dogs followed me everywhere, so I knew I had made new friends.

I explored the hill, crossing a wire fence near a dam, and ventured around the stunted trees on the slopes. Were these the South West Slopes of New South Wales? Not literally. I stopped and watched the autumn sun slide down the western sky; and surveyed the land and imagined it was all mine. A short while later, the injury I escaped could have been mine, when, in the half-light, I jogged back down, forgot the fence, and went flying.

I carted in my backpack and left it in a back bedroom. I twigged it had belonged to a teenage daughter. The room was as you'd expect a room to be, with old 1980s photos of friends on the walls and little accoutrements and reminders all around. I felt sad as the young girl had lost her life in a car accident 25 years ago, and this room had been left as a shrine to her busy life.

The homestead was rustic and comfortable. There was an enclosed back verandah (with a spare TV), and bookcases, and a single area divided into a formal dining area and TV area. I decided I'd eat at a little table in the kitchen.

A back door next to an old Westinghouse refrigerator led through a pantry area to a laundry room and back door. Through the window I could see an old concrete tank in the yard, and I could tell that it had been used as a swimming pool. Next to the laundry was a storage room, and I found shelves packed from head to foot with jars containing nuts, seeds, preserves, oils; and aerosols—fly spray, WD40 and Aeroguard. When you live in the country, you don't generally head to the shops on the way back from work.

I turned on the television knowing full well I'd be accosted with Rugby, not AFL, and this perked me up. The bruise coming up on my knee was coming along nicely, but soon forgotten, and the dogs deserved a well-earnt pat.

CHAPTER 52 SHEARING

In the morning, I used up the last of a loaf of bread, and found butter and preserves in the refrigerator. I took my plate out onto the verandah with the dogs, looking out across the garden.

I looked up when I heard a squeal of brake pads and the sound of worn springs, and saw a young man pull up in a ute at the front door.

"Steve? It's Sam. G'Day mate."

This was the farmer's son who lived ten kilometres down the road checking on me—I expected him.

"Good to see you mate," I said. He replied,

"I've got three-hundred acres I run with my wife. Come over for dinner tonight. I'll take you around here, now, then we'll drop over to mine as I need to check my lambs."

I jumped in the passenger side, and the dogs jumped up for the ride; I may have interrupted their routine, but now they had a new master.

We headed down the track and into fields. Sam pointed out sheep and cows that had issues he'd been keeping an eye on: here I saw one with a limp, there was one with a sore. A section down a steep incline needed a cautious pace. Every time we halted, the dogs followed us to the sheep or cows, tails wagging, tongues hanging out.

The road to Sam's was tarmac for a few kilometres, then continued on compacted dirt. Their house came up alongside a paddock full of sheep.

Sam said, "We're here mate, now you know where to find us."

"Thanks, Sam."

The sheep milled all around us.

"Good prices at the moment, Steve, we need to get these to market. Let's head back. When you come back tonight, watch out for the roos on the road."

Sam looked like a busy man: not only did he look after his own small farm, and have young children like me, but he had a full-time job at a bank in Wagga where he swapped a t-shirt or flannel shirt for a rather more business-like cotton one, and sat tied to a desk.

We jumped on the ute and tore back to the homestead. We spent an hour in the field tearing off silage and laying it out for the cows. It was smelly and dusty as the pieces came apart in our hands. He suddenly looked up:

"Mate. Do you know who you remind me of?"

"Who?" I gasped, out of breath.

"Daniel Craig, the Bond actor."

Well, I never.

I retraced our route to his place in my ute with his advice ringing in my ears.

"Watch out for the roos, they jump out both sides." I craned forward in my seat and looked left and right looking for a telltale shape or movement. It wasn't yet twilight, so the risk was less than if I had left later.

Sam's wife opened the fly screen and greeted me with their small children. She served lamb and veggies for dinner, and Sam and I cracked open some beer stubbies. The lad from the regions and the lad from Melbourne were getting on like a house on fire. He shared with me the time he attended college in the UK.

"Steve did you know I went to Oxford?"

"No, I didn't," I replied, raising an eyebrow and taking a sip from a long neck. This turned out to be an agricultural college in Oxfordshire Sam attended in his early twenties.

"So not exactly Christchurch, then?" I snorted.

We roared with laughter. In fact, we were getting on so well, the rest of the night turned into an exchange of insults and wisecracks.

"Do you two want to get a room?" Sam's wife said from the kitchen.

On my return, I maintained my speed up on the dusty tracks to the farmhouse but kept an eagle eye out for the telltale sign of a roo feeding on the verges. I hadn't come all that way only to come a cropper on a back road.

***

Jobs done, the next day, I lounged in the homestead. My mobile rang, reminding me I had reception.

"Is this Steve Malins?" said the caller.

"It is," I replied. "How can I help?"

"It's New South Wales Police."

My heart raced for a moment. *What's this?*

"Ah—we had a patrol car out on the highway near Lockhart. We had you speeding," said the policeman.

It was obviously Sam, and I knew his game. He sat at work with his banking mates, and he had the opportune moment to have a laugh and a joke at the city lad from town, now he's away from his home turf and in the country. The thing was; I *was* bowling along at a fair lick on the way up. *It was true.*

I showed up at the shearing sheds and jostled with Sam over his practical joke. I found the scene set ready for work and was at once transported back seven years to the last time I had stepped on the boards. Then I had to clamber into a pen with sheep and administer each with a dose of anti-worm treatment, which would see them disease-free through the year.

This was less hard-core, and there were only several hundred to do, and all I had to do was sweep the cuttings from the floor. My city hands let me down when I discovered I had blisters. This sent Sam into fits of laughter. In his eyes I remained the city boy.

After a lazy lunch—reheated lamb chops—and thinking about the route back to Melbourne, I kicked around with the dogs when I noticed water pooling on the ground near a standpipe. Plunging my hands into the pool, I felt a union had failed on a riser pipe. I walked around in circles until the solution presented itself. A bandage rigged with duct tape found in the shed did the job. I called Sam and told him he'll need to swing by and check. He thanked me and had one last thing to say.

"You'd make a bloody good farm manager, mate."

To return to Melbourne, I took the Hume Highway, back over Black spur to the lowland. I drove down our road, and saw they'd had rain that last week, and for the first time in six months, I saw green grass on the nature strip, shiny and squeaky clean. It was pleasing to see.

The Millennial drought had finally broken. I don't think it has ever been as dry.

CHAPTER 53 SKIING THE HIGH PLAINS

"**S**now down to 1,300 metres," said a bloke at work. He was in the kitchen at work talking to a colleague.

It was one of those kitchens in sleek, melamine, put in as part of a recent refurbishment.

"It's going to be bellbird up there on the Sunday," his colleague replied.

I realised I had overheard two Victorians talking about their planned snow trips. I knew also they would be off in their Subarus to resorts on a Friday night, driving non-stop, halting once for a coffee at the servo on the way up.

It came as a surprise to people Australia was skiable, right after the first shock it even snowed here.

The highest peaks of the Alpine received good snow cover in winter. Snow fell from May to September, which meant mountain peaks supported ski industries for a few months.

The seasons were short and took a while to get going. In some years, early snow melted, but larger systems dumped snow in July to form a base. The official opening weekend of the season was the Queen's Birthday weekend, in June, with the Monday a public holiday. Enthusiasts headed for their chalets to greet the start regardless of whether snow had been forecast.

On the other hand, people prized a good dump of snow in September, the first week of spring. On the Main Range in New South Wales, you could ski off-piste into October in good years.

It cost the earth though, that was the thing. Australians paid through the nose. A ski-lift pass was over $100, and hire was another $50 a day. Australian snow was not only unreliable, but it softened in the afternoons and iced up in the shade. I caught an edge a lot on the icy upper slopes in the shadows. You could opt to go further afield to New Zealand to get higher altitudes and more reliable snow, but that wasn't cheap either. Japan was also a destination for Australians hunting snow. People loved it for the powder, the culture, the food, and hospitality; maybe the quirkiness.

We had another low-key mountain to the south at Baw Baw, with little runs which amounted to downhill for those who wanted unfussed skiing a day's trip from the city.

Kiki and I had a look our first winter. *Were we really going to find snow?* We drove up on the main M1 highway to country Gippsland out past the fledging vineyards and farms. After an hour, we took a turnoff towards Noojee—past the well-known pub seen on t-shirts everywhere. We spent an age driving up the bends, winding our way up. It seemed incredible we'd find snow at all, but our doubts were smashed when we hit the snowline.

It had been tamed by a snow plough parked nearby, but snow it was. Kiki fancied ski lessons. We both hired gear, and I left her with her instructor. I asked the nearest liftie where the run was, and he pointed with an outstretched arm.

I was soon making my run down. It was in fact like riding a bike: I hadn't forgotten. I hoped to time my nice wide, skidding hockey stop just as Kiki stood at the bottom with her instructor so I could show off a bit. But I saw her nowhere. I tracked her to the magic carpet and saw she was doing ok.

"Where's the main run mate?" I asked the liftie.

"That was it, mate," he replied.

I couldn't complain, we were a few hours from home, and had a gorgeous day—bellbird conditions. Later Kiki and I stopped in the main village to the car park at a viewpoint. It looked stellar; we could see all the way from the snow line down past snow gums through the green bush to the valley floor. It wasn't cheap, but I knew I would be back one day.

***

1,800 metres. Seems low, I thought, clicking into my bindings at the lift. I'd stayed down in resorts in France at this altitude and skied at twice the altitude.

The piste stretched before me, and a natural bowl sheltered me. Other skiers fussed over gear, but I was ready. Another day of perfect conditions and I was glad of my sunglasses. I'd just been on the phone to a workmate, but I didn't mind the interruption.

We'd dug out an unused credit card and taken the kids away for a week's ski at Mount Hotham seven hours from Melbourne. Most of the resort was above most of the pistes, so you could ski down off the road. The last lifts back up to get to the chalet (or the pub) were 4:30 pm.

It cost a fortune, yes: I rued I could rip up fifty-dollar notes at home without getting cold or a wet bottom. At least we had something to show for it. It helped we had the use of a club lodge with friends, and we could self-cater at nights. I sprung a sticky date pudding on the group one night, and with a topping added by a mum it was a success. We put the kids into ski-school—another expense we tried not to baulk at—and skied all day.

I loved seeing the kids ski. A big hill overlooked the resort, with a large super highway of a run, rated "green". The kids went up the lift and skied on their own. In the mornings, they could ski an access path from the chalet to the lift area. It was funny seeing them descend in helmets, unfettered without poles.

Did I mention the cost? Hot chips were a way of saving cash at lunch. Sometimes sitting around was better than the skiing. One day, we were just getting comfy, and no one wanted to move for the time being. The noise of a helicopter disrupted the silent and happy scene as it came into land whilst we were contemplating another coffee.

"That's the Falls helicopter," said someone, as we all craned to see.

So, rather than drive the two hours through the valley, you could hop on the helicopter to the other resort across the ridge and be there in minutes. Falls Creek was nicknamed "Flat Creek" because of the unchallenging nature of the runs. Advanced Hotham snobs scoffed at it unless you could flit between the two.

CHAPTER 54 TOURING

Touring was definitely *"the go"*, too: skiing out the side of resorts to the back country.

Fall's Creek, where the helicopter flew, perched on the edge of an Alpine feature called the Bogong High Plains above the tree line, a wilderness rolling area. It went on for miles, undulating and barren. The skiing might have been scoffed at, but the side country was *good*.

Skiers set out from the resort for the day with a daypack, Personal Locator Beacon and emergency blanket before returning. The more intrepid headed out to camp out on the plains, with larger packs, four season tent, and sleeping bag.

It was even possible to ski to Mount Hotham following the route the helicopter took. If you were up for it, you'd need to cover twenty kilometres: undulating flats for part of the way, but a nasty steep section into a valley at the end before an epic climb back up to the Hotham car park. You needed to travel light to make the distance, but not get caught out past sunset.

That was for the people who couldn't afford the helicopter, like me. But, I was up for the snow camping.

Harrietville is an Alpine village in the mountains at 500 metres, with a pub, caravan site and a ski-hire outfit. The road climbs to Mount Hotham where we'd skied. It is an hour of mountain road which snakes up 1,000 metres out of the village, and the views are breathtaking, with vistas all the way across the Alpine. The drop on one side is alarming, best not to think about it—and snow chains are needed if snow settles. By the time the road nears the resort the faces look shear, the tops glisten with snow, and the range opposite is seen as a panorama.

A hut called the Diamantina sits by the side of the road as it completes its meander to the resort. This hut is a jump-off point for a track across the ridgeline.

The Razorback track is a prime-time route across the roof of the Victorian High Country, a track to the second highest peak in Victoria, Mount Feathertop. It's an afternoon of walking in summer, longer in winter. It is not demanding—the route rolls up and down, and into glades. I've seen people ski off-track into the gullies on either side.

In 2009, Tim Holding, a government minister, went missing when he got disoriented in low visibility and ended in a gully. It made the front page of the *Herald Sun*, and anyone in an office sweepstake might have taken odds he wasn't going to make it back alive. My manager asked me:

"What do you reckon, Steve?"

"I don't fancy his chances," I said.

After several miserable nights out, rescue came when he was spotted by a TV channel news helicopter.

I looked forward to walking it with two people, one a gnarly looking outdoorsman with a shock of wavy hair, looking every inch like an action hero, and his mate wanting to tag along.

With the sun high in the sky glistening off the névé snow crystals it was always going to be stunning. Every time I stopped to catch breath, adjust a zip, or tighten a crampon strap, I spun around and looked up and down—whichever way I looked, I could see the glare of the land and the azure sky. My trip partner walked ahead, looking the business, making progress head down, breathing hard, lost in his own world.

We made good work of it, but the mate proved slower across the ground. We waited for him to catch up, but it was more time to stand and glory in the sunshine.

We set up in a tiny clump of snow gums near Mount Feathertop in the high ground, but well off the track, out of sight. Hoar snow, or shards glistened when we exposed them with our snow shovels. We lounged around in the evening sunshine as it slanted low and admired the view. The sky was a rust-orange, and wisps of cold air swirled halfway up the mountains, and little winds sprung up and departed, the sound of them whistling through the bowl we had found. The snow gums were stark, but the area down the bottom a vivid green.

But we needed to erect the tent. The pegs used for tents don't work in the snow, so we used longer stakes. It helped if you had sun, lots of it. It made the days far more enjoyable providing we took sunscreen.

"Isn't it amazing?" said my mate. He looked down and had some advice for me:

"Keep your stuff dry, Steve," he said.

It was vital to keep clothing dry, and snow-free, as snowmelt made things wet. If a sleeping bag inside a tent, we'd get chilled and miserable.

We had fun digging a snow kitchen. An expert could dig a trench system from the tent to a kitchen area, a place to sit on the snow with a trench for your legs and feet in twenty minutes. A berm created with the excavated snow kept any wind from the site. Once I saw it done, the penny dropped.

When we were done, my mate offered me a swig. "Want a tot?"

There was room in his pack for the small goon sacks of wine he'd pulled out of a box of dry red. The mate told me once it snowed heavily, leaving his tent under six inches of snow by morning.

A major challenge was getting up in the night to pee. Hardcore users took in water bottles. I fumbled the zip, found my boots and stumbled outside to the snow. The moon was up, and I am not entirely exaggerating when I say it felt like day—all around me lit in the most glorious way. At times like this, I found standing alone in the mountains in the dead of night spiritual.

The hardest part of snow camping had to be getting out of your sleeping bag in the morning. I found it easier if the sun was up. We left the tent out after breakfast to dry, and hung our sleeping bags on snowgum branches too, to air. I reckon, though, the best bit after coming down off the mountain had to be he first hot, fresh coffee in town. And that was only marred when someone took off their boots in the car, and a new aroma reached our nostrils.

CHAPTER 55 HARRY'S PROPERTY

I came to love the High Country, and the rolling hillside and plains we drove to get there.

I'll never forget my first drive there. Melbournians often took the Hume Highway on a Friday night after work, and you could make it there in good time if you left work early.

There is a large *servo* on the highway about two and a half hours north of Melbourne. It is near the town of Glenrowan where the bushranger bandit Ned Kelly had his last stand and is known as Glenrowan services. He wouldn't have understood fast food in the shape of the "Maccas" (MacDonalds) on both sides of the highway, northbound and southbound, even if his draw was similarly fast.

People heading to Albury on the border an extra hour up the road, or heading to the mountains or vineyards stop here, and it's *the* place to stop to stretch your legs. It's a place to people-watch, too.

Over the years, I've seen busy locals, possibly of an agricultural bent, or tradies in shorts. There are people visiting family—dress: as fashion dictates. In winter, skiers dressed in immaculate matching, *après-ski* attire; it's the mums off to Hotham who will be trying the hardest. They don't ski, but they will be proud of their ski-bunny status and looking forward to chucking their kids into ski-school and enjoying a spa or massage whilst hubby skies with his mates.

And there are the sportsmen—the mountain bikers in fleeces and shells; and finally, the destitute look of the hikers, maybe a bit whiffy, too, if they are on the way back home.

My favourite, though, are the young lads who have been tempted to get into the High Country-aesthetic—they prefer a jacked-up ute with all-terrain tyres; raised suspension, a swag on the flat-bed back and will augment their *Blundies* (boots) and shorts with a muscle t-shirt or a check shirt. Maybe a cattleman's hat if they are daring.

The Alpine Way proceeds to the mountains. The more evocative Snow Road is a shortcut, and you can jump on as soon as you leave the services, providing you don't miss the turn. It travels as straight as a Roman road, and many miles of it are through flat plains with glades of trees, the mountains always visible in the distance. Vineyards sited along the way tempt people to stop. The best time to visit is on a temperate day in autumn when the colours are at their most florid. The road joins the Alpine Way, and motorists merge back into the congo line of traffic that proceeds to the mountains.

Mrytleford is a town with a large migrant Italian population. It's a stock country town with cafes and supermarkets. Many people don't stop, and shoot straight through, just ensuring they observe the speed limit in case a police car is hidden behind a rise. Bright is another alpine mountain gateway, the sort of place city people enjoy getaways. The same people might hit the trails on mountain-bikes in the area in summer. Girls with down puffer jackets with fur-trim collars walk around with a coffee extended in one arm.

I travelled these highways many times over the years, and whilst the hours of the Hume were tiresome, the allure of the hills never lessened.

***

We had a friend who owned a farm tucked away in the hills behind Mrytleford out of the way of the punters.

It was 500 acres, larger than a hobby farm, but not in the big league. Our friend was a cockie, a hard grafter and owner who just about turned a profit. He loved the lifestyle. Cockies don't send their kids to boarding schools nor own top of the range Land Cruisers.

Harry loved the land, the opportunity. He grew up in the Ovens valley, a real-life character from Bryce Courtenay's *Four*

Fires novel set in the valley towns. Chinese migrants worked his land during the 19th century, and he loved the idea of the history. He ran cattle and sheep. The farmhouse, a small two-bed cottage was reached by a dirt driveway 300m long which meanders slightly, as if lost, before straightening to meet a gate.

Walking in the frost one winter's morning, we found two large dams and a small plantation of newly planted trees. The ground rose to a tree line one side of the property with stellar views. Curious cows stood in shelter out of the wind. Next to the farmhouse lay a huge gum tree which threw shade over shedding containing a small Suzuki 4wd and an early model Land Cruiser. I took a look. Whilst a man's house might be his castle, his shed is an insight into his very soul.

I found a handsome Kawasaki dirt bike and a workbench full of dirt and dust with miscellaneous hardware. In the regions, people don't have immaculate tooling and gear—they are too busy working to spend all their hours cleaning or tidying. There's no Mr Jones next door to impress. My feet were freezing, so we headed to the warmth of the kitchen where a real wood fire burnt.

"Want a cup of tea?" Harry asked.

"Yes, please," we replied, in unison.

He is a character; a man hewn by life outside and in the regions. This is not a city boy or suburban man, but someone who had taken every opportunity that come his way. He had seen the harder years along with the easier ones.

"I don't work too hard though, these days," he said with a wry grin, as he added oregano to a pot of lamb stew.

He wanted to look at his cows and invited us to come with him. I jumped next to him on the tractor and the kids clambered on, finding a handheld. Now here was a chance of injury—I hoped they wouldn't come to grief. The young calves looked at us with silly, lazy eyes and didn't seem at all bothered by us turning up on their turf. I could see why people think they are cute.

As night fell, Harry persuaded me to help him shoot foxes.

We weren't apologetic for the chase. They were after the lambs in the paddocks and needing dispatching to their maker. This wasn't the dubious activity of racing across the local landscape on horseback following the hounds as in the UK. It had been banned around the time we arrived in Australia. This was taking aim through the iron sights of an old .22 rifle. The rounds Harry handed over were tiny, not much bigger than the air rifle pellets I had bought in the UK.

I laid in the prone position outside the farmhouse and got the rifle in my shoulder to get a sense of the weight and balance. The stock was old and had lots of dings and scratches, and the trigger had been worn smooth by countless fingers.

The mode of transport was not on foot but in Harry's 4x4 wagon, and I made myself comfortable in the passenger seat whilst he drove the rises and dips of the property to the high ground.

I rested the barrel of the rifle through the open window. Above us, a half-moon which gave just enough light to see the undulations of the landscape. Kiki had stayed back in the kitchen by the fire. The kids meanwhile sat in the back and winced every time I lined up for the shot.

"Dad! You had *better* miss," said Miss Eldest.

"We'll see…" I mouthed.

She had misunderstood the farmer's mission.

They blocked their ears when I pulled the trigger, being careful not to snatch or pull. I didn't want to miss.

But miss I did. I had not sighted the rifle for my eye, and at the range we found our quarry, it was an uphill struggle. The headlights of the ute found the fox alright, but at something like 200 metres. Wedged against the door, I had precious seconds to get my rifle in my shoulder, brace myself, acquire a decent sight picture and squeeze off the shot. I hoped Harry would not move the vehicle and disturb my aim.

Crack!

The sound of the round exiting the barrel at 500 feet per second was not deafening but loud enough to cause the kids to cower on the back seat. Every time I missed, they smiled. Every time I cursed, they cheered. Every time a furry predator bolted and slunk away; they were grateful.

Back at the farmhouse, we sunk into leather couchettes and Harry stoked the kitchen open fire from a wooden chair. The flames shot up the chimney, the hearth stones blackened. The wood spat and crackled. Kiki uncoiled her scarf.

"Want a cuppa?" he asked.

CHAPTER 56 IN YACK

The main street of Yackandandah, or "Yack" was typical of the region, catering to a local population and a crowd of weekend "blow-ins". An assortment of essentials: local independent supermarket, newsagent, but also clothes boutiques.

This was rounded out by three antique shops which provided amusement to the Melbourne city blow-ins. We looked around, careful not to knock anything over. There were records, china, metal toys, an old ancient radio and scale models of aeroplanes and boats.

We came to know the delis and bakeries. People sat at tables with their morning coffee and a cake—a muffin, or a custard tart—dressed in their finest High Country rural chic. If this wardrobe was not available, they dressed in outback chic: flannel shirt, rugged shorts and a pair of *Blundstones*. They had made the movie *Strange Bedfellows* here, but there were no cameras to be seen.

Beechworth close by was another Yackandandah, only arranged at a larger scale with even more "Ye Olde World" boutiques, many selling knitwear to appeal to a genteel crowd who want to eschew manmade fibres and look the part, in merino, or possum fur. The town is set on two roads, one marginally busier than the other, and at the crossroads we admired an imposing post office. The Anglican church of bluestone reminded me it had been there for over a century close on 150 years.

Melbournians flock to the site of a well-known bakery, a stop on their travels in the region. There's always a queue in the shop. People are prepared to wait a bit longer for a pie with a filling of their choice after three hours on the Hume Highway from Melbourne.

And I always made sure the kids' hands were safely out of the way when we sauntered around the shops selling knick-knacks that never seemed to sell anything, nor turn a profit.

One Labour Day weekend in March, we visited friends in Kooyong near the border with New South Wales. The river Murray formed the border. The town was larger than I had thought, and I marvelled at the produce in the independent stores and the eccentric hardware in shops as we browsed. I bought a lock knife I knew would barely see use but might get sharpened once a decade.

We found our friends camped in a spot out in the bush, a home away from home. The campsite was out of sight and undiscoverable to park rangers. Through a gap in the trees, we found an entire setup of tables, tents, even a kitchen area on the banks of the river. It looked like a film set from *Out of Africa*.

I noted a large cast-iron pot on a wood fire with a leg of lamb cooking in its own juices, with vegetables, lid on. It needed little attention, or fixing, and the joint stewed away slowly for hours. A dilapidated jetty overlooked the water. Old rubber tyres had been left there, and the kids used them as rafts in the river. When they discovered the border was the *river*, they took great delight in setting off, drifting downstream to spin in an eddy, and land on the opposite bank—where they could claim to have gone inter-state. They carried the tube on the New South Wales shore and paddled back to their home state in Victoria.

The lamb was a bushman's dream and pronounced ready just before sunset.

The new day was forecast to be a scorcher, but I saw everyone looked keen to visit a race gathering at Towong Racecourse, the next town along. Country people love a day out and will drive a long way for a festival or gathering, whether a wedding, or even a Bachelor & Spinster Party set up in a paddock. The racetrack was used in the 1980s movie *Phar Lap*, the champion New Zealand horse race adored by an Australian public.

We turned off the highway in a cloud of dust and headed

alongside the racetrack to a grandstand. Beer tents touted for business—hospitality was turning a dollar here. Thankfully, large elm trees provided shade from the blinding sun behind the grandstand.

The racehorses were well-watered and shaded in a holding area. Stable girls walked the horses by admiring punters, their thoroughbred conditioned bodies slick in the sunshine. Everyone was dressed to the nines in race or country clobber: flowery dresses, twill shirts, chino trousers and RM Williams boots, and the Akubra hat made an appearance on men and women of all ages. It was a fine place to be on an autumn day, and to have a glass of chilled Sauv Blanc away from town.

CHAPTER 57 DID WE FIND WHAT WE WERE LOOKING FOR?

The deer hunter looked at me and smiled.

"We like it mate, it's part of a tradition. It gets into your blood. I can understand why people disapprove, though. I respect that." He looked down respectfully.

I nodded, and glanced past his elbow to a long sliver which broke his silhouette. It was a '30-06 Sako bolt-action rifle slung over his shoulder. He unslung it and showed me. I saw it was unloaded—no sign of a magazine, but he showed me the chamber so I could be sure. He wore green camouflage, in a breathable mesh cloth, sleeves rolled up. Atop his head was a saturated blaze-orange cap.

"We need to be seen," he explained.

What had brought me face to face with this hunter?

I had joined a bush walking club which sent volunteers out to look for missing people. We were called before the media were alerted and the story was all over the news. Hikers got lost in impenetrable terrain, and we specialised in supporting the various search agencies, including the police, bringing in numbers to augment manpower. Often, we were tasked to head into deep ravines and dense gullies. Police, and the families were grateful for extra boots on the ground.

A deer hunter had gone missing last year, and this was one way of their community getting to know us, maybe a little "PR", as we had turned out to look for one of their own.

Hunting is a serious business in Australia, and guns are big business in Australia. I had spotted shooting magazines in the waiting room of the doctors, and these were as much about pests as deer or other game. A few of the people in the magazine looked *savage,* but some had a larrikan twinkle in their eye.

There had long been a relationship between animals and the High Country. Not long after we settled in Melbourne, the state government had just allowed pastoralists to introduce cattle for grazing, after a ban for years. The environmentalists had a distinct opposition due to damage and soil erosion. They agreed to disagree, but bumper stickers on cars and utes told the pastoralists side:

Cattle men care for the High Country.

But back to searching. Just like the Country Fire Authority, we were on 24/7 call.

Most of the searchers were seasoned bush walkers, competent map readers and off-track navigators. They were self-supporting for up to three nights, so could be dropped off somewhere. When the call came, we could grab a pack and be on the ground in 12 hours. Pickup was an early start from key police stations around Melbourne.

We trained in snow rescue techniques on skis and snowshoes, with ropes, harnesses, snow stakes and avalanche gear.

The snowpack in the Australia Alps is dangerous. The marginal conditions, and freeze-melt caused layers of unstable snow to form, and entire slabs can give way in what's known as a "slab release". The steepest slopes are the most dangerous. A skier can safely traverse a slope only for it to release and bury companions later. In 2014, two skiers died on Mount Bogong and the team were required to recover them.

One year, the team filed up Mount Bogong on a Saturday to train in the snow at the top. I wore my ski boots the first parts of the dirt until we hit the snow line and donned snowshoes.

We set up camp in the drifts near Mitchell hut and cached our gear. It was labourious climbing to the top of the mountain. Unlike Mount Feathertop, the summit wasn't a traditional dramatic peak but a sloping hill. On a different day, we'd see miles, but the visibility was low. We dug ice pits to examine the snowpack to get insights into avalanche behaviour, then moved to an easier slope out of danger to practice self-arrest.

One by one, we hurled ourselves down the slope and dug our axes into the slope to halt our slide.

A shout came from the bottom, and all eyes flitted towards it.

"I've done my leg in!" called one of the guys.

"Let's take a look." One of the medics climbed down to see.

He had broken his ankle post-holing in his boots in the deep snow. In between wincing with the pain, he was angry to let the team down.

So, the training exercise turned into a real-life rescue. A police helicopter flew in during the night, and we lit the area with our head-torches, but the rescue crew couldn't get close enough through cloud to winch him up.

Sunday dawned bright, and we carried our gear half-way down the mountain and climbed back to stretcher him. It was several hours of hauling and carrying, over logs and around gnarly corners, taking it in turns to haul the stretcher. The helicopter returned and circled above looking for a gap in the trees. A police rescuer was lowered onto the track, and they winched him up. All we had to do: retrieve our gear and begin the march to the car park.

I thought it a relief to get back to Melbourne—and home.

CHAPTER 59 LESSONS LEARNT

It has now been 21 years since I arrived in the Great Southern Land, and 18 since we married. My children are all teenagers and my eldest is learning to drive on her "L" plates, with my youngest daughter about to take a theory test and get hers. My son is still the proficient footballer and basketball player, and sidesteps players or swings around defenders easily, with his long blond locks flying behind him.

Covid impacted us like many. After an initial six-week lockdown which saw, frankly, many families enjoy the new working conditions, and a chance to avoid the commute, we were released. But infections arose. We were locked down over winter by the State government, amongst the longest lockdowns anywhere in the world. Our State Premier imposed a curfew past 8 pm. It looked like he was chasing zero infections, or "doughnuts". The office I had built came in handy when we were both working or studying. Restrictions were eased from a five-kilometre radius to 20k, whilst we waited for cases to decline. Then we did it all again the next winter, when restrictions came back.

We have achieved a lot as a family. We brought up bi-lingual children and made seven trips to the US and Mexico. I calculated my daughter had crossed the vast ocean 14 times by the age of 16. That might be more air miles than I've ever done. I got back to London twice, with two baby girls, and then three teenagers and rejoiced in the fact they got to see the Houses of Parliament, Big Ben and the Changing of the Guard at Buckingham Palace just before the Queen passed later that year.

We continued to fix up the house: we restored the roof and landscaped the front garden. There is always something to do in Melbourne or surrounds, a mixture of city and country-living. The standard of living is high: there's a reason Australian house prices are some of the highest in the world. It's a destination of choice along with Canada. We can't complain and wouldn't change anything.

And what came of the firefighter who fell through the roof of the house fire that autumn night? He died of cancer before Covid after a short illness. Sadly, our captain and a fellow firefighter also passed before the pandemic, in the line of proud people who served the local community and have their names immortalised on the station walls.

A YEAR ON LAND AND SEA

[The No #1 Best seller]

Have you ever parachuted in the moonlight and juggled work with play? In 1995, Steve was trying to figure out how to take a degree, keep up with his military training, and learn to sail in spring Scottish waters. He couldn't say no to an invitation to sail across the Atlantic when St Lucia and the Caribbean were the prize.

It's hard enough keeping a romance alive when there were distractions like landing a gig as a swordsman on a Hollywood movie. There were other commitments—a jaunt to Pamplona in

Spain, rowing in the Swiss lakes, and a camp in the United States, before he could join his crew.

Will he get to the Tropics, have time for a girlfriend, or will he end up in the doldrums? A timeless coming of age story of action, romance and grasping opportunities, as a year unfolded.

Available on Amazon

RAH RAH AND ROOS : FARMING AND TRAVEL IN THE GREAT SOUTHERN LAND

Is it time you ditched the office and headed to the outback of Australia for the adventure of a lifetime? In 2002, a young Englishman left London behind to do just that.

One year, 2,000 sheep: 4,000 km travelled. Horses and quad bikes. Two light aircraft, one Ford station wagon. He uncovered real life far from the hustle and bustle of the beaches and coffee shops of the East coast. There were "Skimpies", surly farmers and tough miners, vets and call-girls. He was ready for the flying lessons but not quite ready to take a test in a ten-tonne truck, and almost came a cropper in the gold fields in 40-degree heat.

A must-read for anyone following in the finest traditions of travel "Down Under" who wants to read travel with a twist.

Available on Amazon

ACKNOWLEDGEMENT

I'd like to thank Chris Moore, Simon Michael Prior, Jacqueline Maude and Alison Ripley-Cubitt for their assistance with my manuscript, and all those who can't be, (or would rather not be) named for their kind encouragement. Also, to my darling wife Kiki, and children, who put up with my excitement and talking about it too much, as yet another book took shape some 30 years after events.

ABOUT THE AUTHOR

Years later, Steve now lives in Melbourne, Australia, with his wife and three teenagers. As such, he is an unpaid uber-driver. He works in an office for his many sins, but volunteered as a Country Fire Authority firefighter and loves getting out in the High Country and on skis in the Australian Alps.

Printed in Dunstable, United Kingdom